AN ALBUM OF
WORLD WAR II

BY DOROTHY AND
THOMAS HOOBLER

FRANKLIN WATTS | NEW YORK | LONDON | 1977

Cover design by Nick Krenitsky

Photographs courtesy of: National Archives: p. 61 (bottom); National Archives/U.S. Office of War Information: pp. 6 (top and left), 34, 66, 67, 76 (bottom), 79 (top), 86 (bottom), 91; National Archives/U.S. Coast Guard: p. 6 (bottom); National Archives/U.S. Information Agency: pp. 11, 12, 16, 23 (center left and right, bottom), 31; National Archives/Collection of Foreign Records Seized 1941: p. 49; National Archives/Navy Department: pp. 33 (top), 36, 39, 86 (top left); Franklin D. Roosevelt Library: pp. 10, 13, 25, 33 (bottom), 37, 42 (left and bottom), 45, 47, 69 (bottom), 73, 84, 85 (right); U.S. Army: pp. 15, 17, 19, 35, 40, 62, 64, 69 (top), 74, 75, 78, 79 (bottom), 80 (top and bottom), 83 (top), 85 (left), 86 (top right), 88, 89; Netherlands State Institute for War Documentation: p. 18; Imperial War Museum: pp. 20 (top), 23 (top), 24, 50, 56 (top), 72 (top and bottom); Radio Times Hulton Picture Library: p. 20 (center); French Embassy Press & Information Division: pp. 20 (bottom), 44; Sovfoto: pp. 26 (top and bottom), 53 (top and bottom), 54, 55, 76 (top); United Press International: pp. 30, 48; U.S. Navy: p. 56 (bottom); U.S. Air Force: pp. 38, 60, 61 (top), 63, 83 (bottom), 93 (left and bottom); Kodansha International Ltd.: pp. 41, 93 (top); The Bettmann Archive: p. 42 (top right); Defense Department/Marine Corps.: pp. 46, 90; U.S. Coast Guard: p. 58; Collection, The Museum of Modern Art, New York: p. 59; Sekai Bunka Publishing Inc.: pp. 80 (left).

Maps courtesy of: Dyno Lowenstein: pp, 29, 51, 54; and Vantage Art, Inc.: pp. 8, 14, 70.

Cover photographs courtesy of: Imperial War Museum: left; National Archives/U.S. Information Agency: right; Defense Department/Marine Corps.: center. page 1: Imperial War Museum.

Library of Congress Cataloging in Publication Data

Hoobler, Dorothy.
    An album of World War II.

    Includes index.

    SUMMARY: The global nature of World War II is described and illustrated with photographs and maps.
    1. World War, 1939–1945—Campaigns—Juvenile literature. [1. World War, 1939–1945—Campaigns] I. Hoobler, Thomas, joint author. II. Title.
D743.7.H66   940.54′002′40544   77–5090
ISBN 0–531–02911–5

CONTENTS

AN ALBUM OF
WORLD WAR II

Right: sometimes the tragedy of war was too much to bear, even for seasoned soldiers. On Okinawa, one U.S. Marine comforts another who broke down and wept after seeing one of his close friends killed in the fighting. Below: in the midst of war, even small victories brought a momentary joy. The elation of these American soldiers shows through their black camouflage paint as they inspect a captured German machine gun nest in Italy.

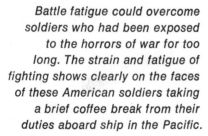

Battle fatigue could overcome soldiers who had been exposed to the horrors of war for too long. The strain and fatigue of fighting shows clearly on the faces of these American soldiers taking a brief coffee break from their duties aboard ship in the Pacific.

INTRODUCTION

World War II was the most destructive war in history. Over 35 million people were killed, and the property damage ran into the hundreds of billions of dollars. Seventy million men and women served in the armed forces of both sides. Millions more participated as resistance fighters in occupied territories.

World War II was truly global. Fifty-seven nations entered the war. In contrast to World War I, which was primarily fought in Europe, World War II reached into Europe, Asia, Africa, and the islands of the Pacific. World War II was in fact two major wars. The Asian war began in China in 1937, and the European war began in Poland in 1939. With the entry of the United States into the war in 1941, the two wars connected in one worldwide struggle.

The war resulted from aggression by Germany and Italy in Europe and Japan in Asia. Later, as the war grew, the "war effort" became the single purpose of the mightiest countries in the world. Civilians who stayed home and worked in the factories were almost as important as soldiers in battle.

Yet the life of any one individual became insignificant as worldwide suffering and death increased. Families were torn apart. Millions of people were driven from their homes and brutalized. Entire countries were overrun and occupied. The most horrifying crime of the war was the Germans' massacre of 6 million Jews. This crime would haunt the memory of the world that survived.

In retrospect, the war may have been won off the battlefield in the factories and laboratories. The greater industrial and scientific strength of the Allies prevailed. Finally, the war gave birth to the ultimate weapon—the atomic bomb. Use of the bomb against Japan brought the war to an end, and changed the nature of all wars to come. The threat of total destruction now hung over the world.

THE EUROPEAN WAR THROUGH 1941

NORWAY

FINLAND

Leningrad

NORTH SEA

SWEDEN

ESTONIA

BALTIC SEA

IRELAND

DENMARK

LATVIA

UNION OF SOVIET
SOCIALIST REPUBLICS

GREAT
BRITAIN

NETHER-
LANDS

Memel

Danzig

LITHUANIA

London

Antwerp

Rotterdam

GERMANY

Berlin

EAST
PRUSSIA

POLAND

Moscow

ATLANTIC OCEAN

English Channel

Dunkirk

Brussels

Rhineland

Warsaw

BELGIUM

Eben
Emael

Sudetenland

Brest-Litovsk

Ardennes Forest

LUX.

CZECHOSLOVAKIA

Ukraine

Bay of Biscay

Paris

Vichy

SWITZ.

AUSTRIA

HUNGARY

Crimea

Sevastapol

RUMANIA

PORTUGAL

YUGOSLAVIA

BLACK SEA

SPAIN

CORSICA

ITALY

Adriatic Sea

BULGARIA

ALBANIA

SARDINIA

SPANISH
MOROCCO

MEDITERRANEAN SEA

GREECE

TURKEY

MOROCCO (FR.)

ALGERIA (FR.)

SICILY

⬚ ⭐ Axis expansion before
the invasion of Poland

THE ROAD TO WAR IN EUROPE

Legacy of World War I

When the victorious Allies sat down at the peace conference at the end of World War I, Europe was devastated. Belgium, large portions of France, and Eastern Europe had seen four years of heavy fighting. The destruction was enormous. The victorious nations, with the exception of the United States, were financially drained. The threat of Communist revolution hung over Eastern Europe. Neither the defeated powers nor the new Communist government of Russia attended the peace conference. It was in this atmosphere that the Treaty of Versailles was written.

By the terms of the Treaty of Versailles, the map of Europe was changed. New nations were created. Germany was allowed to keep most of its territory, but was held responsible for starting the war and had to pay reparations (compensation for war costs) to the victors. The treaty restricted the size of the German army to 100,000 men, and forbade German development of heavy weapons, air power, and large ships. The German people were bitter at this treatment. The new German government, the Weimar Republic, was blamed for accepting the harsh conditions.

Economic hardship in Europe, particularly in Germany, increased after the war. The inflation that struck Germany in 1923 was so great that people brought their money to the markets in wheelbarrows. Britain and France also suffered from hard times. The turnover of governments in France was so rapid that no strong policy was possible. In 1929, the Wall Street crash in the United States triggered an even greater worldwide depression. These conditions led to widespread dissatisfaction with existing governments, and heightened the appeal of Fascism.

The League of Nations was created at the peace conference to settle international disputes and keep the peace. Unfortunately, the United States was kept from joining by its Congress. Germany and the Soviet Union did not join until later. The League was never a strong force.

The terrible destruction of World War I made the victorious Allies determined never to fight again. In the case of the French, this attitude led to a dependence on heavy border fortifications. Fear of attack became the only national defense policy.

The Rise of Fascism

Though Italy had been on the winning side in World War I, it had not shared in the spoils of war. An unimpressive military performance combined with corrupt and weak political leadership created dissatisfaction with the government.

In this climate, a new political leader named Benito Mussolini arose. He offered a vision of a restored Roman Empire. Italians responded to his call, and in 1922 his followers, known as Fascists, marched on Rome and took control of the government.

The Fascists soon suppressed all other political parties, along with workers' unions and other independent groups. Newspapers were censored. The state, through the Fascist party, provided all the news, which aimed at glorifying the state, the party, and Mussolini himself, who was called *Il Duce* (the leader). Independent thought and opposition to Fascism were not tolerated.

Later, Germany followed a similar path. Adolf Hitler led a group called the National Socialists, or Nazis. Hitler played on the dissatisfaction of the German people with the Treaty of Versailles and promised to restore Germany's military greatness. Hitler said the Germans had not really been defeated in 1918, but had been stabbed in the back by traitors at home. Among those traitors, according to Hitler, were the Jews.

Part of Hitler's appeal was his contention that the Germans were a "master race" that should dominate the "inferior" races, such as Jews and Slavs. The Slavic peoples made up much of the populations of countries in Eastern Europe. Hitler said the Germans needed the land in the East as *Lebensraum,* or living space. The Germans were entitled to the use of this land as a "superior" people.

Mussolini called his followers Fascists. In Italian, a fascio *is a bundle of sticks. Mussolini's message was that a single stick breaks easily, but a bundle of them together is strong. Facing page: Like Mussolini, Hitler used mass communications to glorify himself, the Nazi Party, and the state. Huge outdoor rallies used the symbols of Nazism and powerful speakers to produce mob approval.*

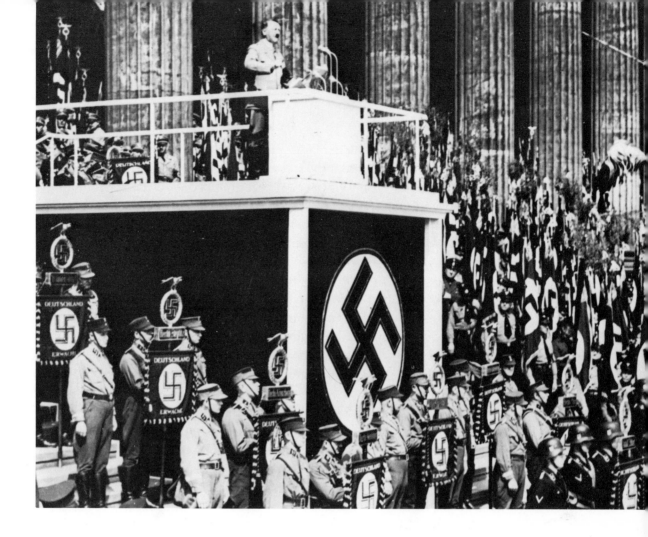

When Hitler came to power, his anti-Jewish campaign deprived Jews of their property and forbade them participation in the professions such as teaching, medicine, and law. Later, the Nazis rounded up the Jews and sent them to concentration camps. By that time, Hitler had stilled the voices of dissent in Germany, as Mussolini had in Italy.

Another part of the Nazi platform was opposition to Communism. Hitler thus gained the crucial support of some German businessmen and military officers who felt they could manipulate Hitler once he came to power. They were mistaken.

Hitler was named chancellor of Germany in 1933. The following year, on the death of President Hindenburg, Hitler assumed full control of the government, taking for himself the title of *Führer,* or leader. Hitler's policies soon seemed to be solving the economic problems of Germany. He began building up the army, without interference from Britain or France. Huge public works projects gave many people jobs. The Germans rallied behind their *Führer.* And the other nations of Europe had little will to stop him.

[11]

The Peace Breaks Down

In 1933, Germany announced it was leaving the League of Nations. Two years later, Germany resumed the conscripting of soldiers, which had been forbidden by the Treaty of Versailles. None of the Allies attempted to enforce the treaty.

Impressed by Hitler's boldness, Mussolini ordered an Italian attack on Ethiopia in October 1935. By the next year, Ethiopia had been overrun. The leader of Ethiopia, Haile Selassie, appealed to the League of Nations for protection. The League censured Italy and imposed an embargo forbidding the shipment of war material to Italy. However, oil was not included in the embargo, and Italy continued its aggression without further interference.

In 1936, Hitler sent his troops into the Rhineland, a part of Germany bordering France. This had been forbidden by the Treaty of Versailles. Again the action went unchallenged.

In July of 1936, a Spanish general named Francisco Franco led his Fascist supporters in revolt against the republican government of Spain. Germany and Italy sent aid to Franco, and the Soviet Union aided the Republicans. The other European countries looked the other way, and Franco triumphed.

Hitler became bolder. In 1938, he exerted pressure on the chancellor of Austria forcing his resignation. German troops entered Austria to "restore order." Austria became part of Germany without a shot being fired.

Destruction in the Spanish Civil War. Italy and particularly Germany used the war as a testing ground for new weapons and fighting techniques. The assistance given to both sides made the war drag on until 1939, resulting in the deaths of over 600,000 Spaniards.

Now Hitler turned to Czechoslovakia, a democratic country that had been created by the Treaty of Versailles. About 3,250,000 citizens of Czechoslovakia were of German descent, living in a region called the Sudetenland. Hitler demanded that the Czechs turn the Sudetenland over to Germany. The Czechs prepared to resist, but in Munich on September 29, 1938, Britain, France, Italy, and Germany met and agreed that the Sudetenland belonged to Germany.

The year 1939 brought more demands from the Axis nations—Germany and Italy. Hitler took the rest of Czechoslovakia, and the city of Memel from Lithuania. Italy seized Albania. Now Hitler began making demands on Poland.

At first, France and Britain gave in to Hitler's demands, but they finally realized that "appeasement" would not stop Hitler. They began to build up their armed forces, but the Germans had a head start. Britain and France turned to the Soviet Union to unite with them against Hitler. But it was too late. The Russian leader, Josef Stalin, realized that Hitler could offer a better deal than the British and French. Hitler made Stalin a secret offer to divide Poland and the Baltic states into German and Russian spheres. The Soviet Union and Germany, the two former ideological archenemies, signed the Nonaggression Pact on August 23, 1939. The world was shocked.

Hitler had made sure he would not have to fight on two fronts. The French and British promised to support Poland if it was attacked. The world waited for Hitler to move.

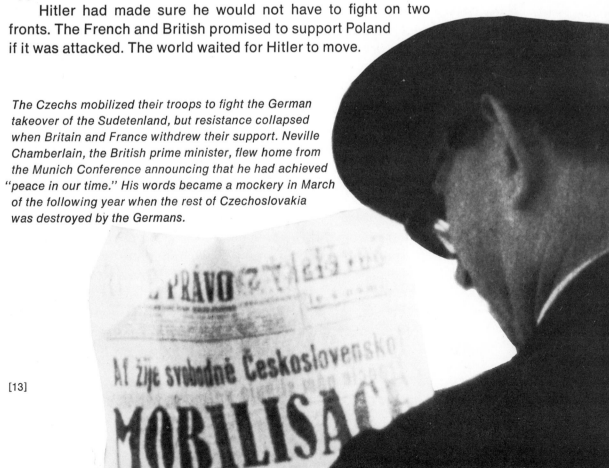

The Czechs mobilized their troops to fight the German takeover of the Sudetenland, but resistance collapsed when Britain and France withdrew their support. Neville Chamberlain, the British prime minister, flew home from the Munich Conference announcing that he had achieved "peace in our time." His words became a mockery in March of the following year when the rest of Czechoslovakia was destroyed by the Germans.

[13]

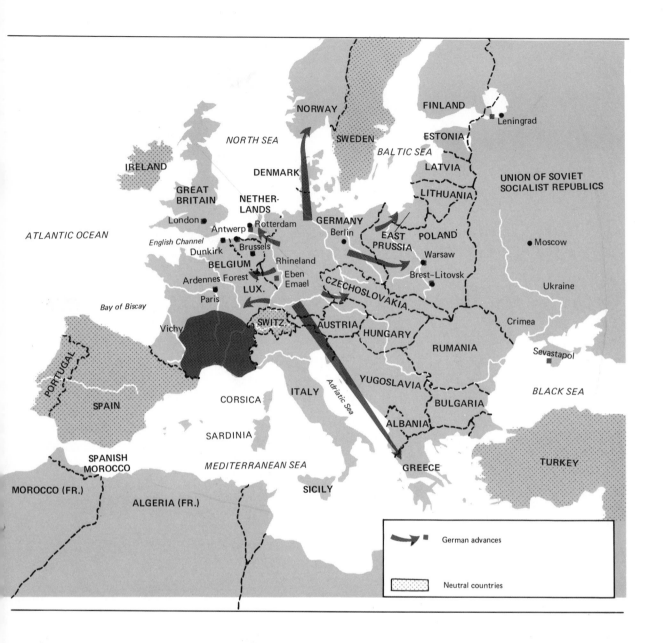

German advances

Neutral countries

FIRST PHASES OF THE WAR

Blitzkrieg in Poland

Shortly after midnight on September 1, 1939, aircraft of the German *Luftwaffe* (air force) flew over the Polish border to bomb Polish cities, airfields, and railroads. The Polish air force was virtually destroyed on the ground. At six that morning Nazi troops crossed the frontier between the two countries. Hitler's troops entered Poland from three directions, including the area that had been Czechoslovakia.

The German strategy was to encircle the defending Polish armies and quickly capture the capital city of Warsaw. Vital communications and supply bases were knocked out. *Panzer* (tank) units crashed through the Polish fortifications. German dive-bombers swooped downward with a frightening sound and deadly accuracy upon civilians and soldiers alike. Then followed the German motorcycle troops, the foot soldiers, and the horse-drawn artillery. The world had never seen military action of such speed and mobility. The attack on Poland was the first of the German *Blitzkriegs,* or lightning wars.

Against the *Blitzkrieg,* the Poles assembled a military force whose strongest units were horse-mounted cavalry. The Polish troops were stationed too far forward, and were overrun before they could retreat to stronger positions.

On September 3, Britain and France declared war on Germany, but they launched no effective attack. Hitler had gambled by leaving the border with France poorly defended, but the French stayed safely behind their border fortifications, called the Maginot Line.

The Soviet Union moved its forces into Poland from the east on the seventeenth of September. The Polish government fled to Rumania the following day, and later exiles set up a government in Paris. Warsaw, the Polish capital, fell on the twenty-seventh, and by October 5, the Germans and Soviets had divided the country between them.

Poland was an ideal testing ground for Hitler's Blitzkrieg. *The flat terrain, with few obstacles such as rivers and forests, made the swift movement of tanks and troops easy. German soldiers, shown here firing on Warsaw, conquered Poland quickly.*

The Winter War

The speed and efficiency of the German attack alarmed even Stalin. He now became concerned that he get all that had been promised by the Nonaggression Pact. The Soviets demanded bases and territorial concessions from the Baltic countries. All but Finland gave in.

On November 30, the Soviets attacked along a broad front across the southern and eastern borders of Finland. The Russian attack was slow and disorganized. Stalin thought the Finns would surrender easily. His planes dropped leaflets on the Finnish towns, urging them not to resist. The Finns fought back, counterattacking on skis, moving swiftly to cut the Russian supply lines. During this fighting, the Finns threw bottles filled with fuel to disable Russian tanks. They called these makeshift bombs "Molotov cocktails," after the Russian foreign minister, Vyacheslav Molotov.

World opinion condemned the Russians. More humiliatingly, the first Soviet attack was unsuccessful. Stalin prepared a second attack. This time, the target was a narrow front along the southern border of Finland, only twenty miles north of the Russian city of Leningrad. The Finnish border fortifications, known as the Mannerheim Line, collapsed under the massive Soviet attack. Finland surrendered on March 12, ceding the territory demanded by the Soviets. Later, the Finns would ally with Germany to regain their lost territory.

In the bitter winter fighting in Finland, many inadequately clothed Russian soldiers froze in the snow. Stalin's difficulty in conquering Finland led him to modernize the Soviet army.

[16]

German soldiers in Norway, riding in a special car used to shoot down saboteurs. The resistance movement in Norway was one of the most effective in any country.

Invasion of Denmark and Norway

After the Germans defeated Poland, the rest of Europe waited fearfully for the dictator's next attack. This period dragged on for months, as Hitler strengthened the German fortifications on the French border, known as the Siegfried Line. Britain and France's inactivity at this time was known as the *Sitzkrieg* (sit-down war), or Phony War. Meanwhile, Hitler prepared his next move.

Germany needed iron ore from Sweden to keep its war machine going. This ore passed by ship through the port of Narvik in Norway. Both Hitler and Britain realized the strategic value of Norwegian ports. British ships began to mine the ports to prevent attack, but it was too late. The next day, April 9, 1940, the German attack began. Hitler seized Narvik and other important Norwegian cities in the first twenty-four hours of fighting. The same day, the Germans invaded and conquered Denmark.

The war in Norway continued, as Norwegian fighters inland harassed the Germans. British and French reinforcements landed in the north of Norway, and Narvik was recaptured on May 28. By that time, however, the war on the mainland of Europe required the transfer of the British and French troops. On their departure, the Germans recaptured Narvik. Norway surrendered completely on June 9.

German paratroopers dropping into Belgium. The Blitzkrieg tactics depended on early and effective air support such as this, along with bombing raids to soften up enemy targets.

THE BATTLE FOR FRANCE

Invasion of the Lowlands

On May 10, Hitler launched the invasion of the lowlands—Luxemburg, The Netherlands, and Belgium. Luxemburg fell the first day. The Netherlands, which had hoped to stay neutral, as it had in 1914, planned to open its dikes to flood the countryside and slow the German advance. Hitler foiled this plan by sending parachutists in advance of his army to capture the key defensive points of the dikes. The *Blitzkrieg* worked again, and the Dutch were defeated in five days. Rotterdam was heavily bombed by the Germans, with 40,000 civilian deaths, as an example to other countries not to resist.

Belgium had been the invasion route that the Germans used to get to France in 1914. Britain and France expected that the same plan would be followed this time. When German troops invaded Belgium, the British and French forces moved to oppose them.

The Ardennes Offensive

Before the war, the French pondered what had gone wrong in 1914. They saw that the Germans could again engage French armies at the eastern border of France while sending the real attack through Belgium to the north. France decided to build a line of fortifications, called the Maginot Line, on the border with Germany. The Maginot Line would be so strong that it could not be broken through. French troops would then be free to meet the invading Germans coming from the north.

But Hitler and his generals had a surprise for the French. They went north of the main strength of the Maginot Line to an area called the Ardennes Forest, in Belgium and France. The French had thought that Hitler's tanks and troops could not move swiftly through the densely wooded Ardennes. But the German *Wehrmacht* (armed forces) proved them wrong. A German army, using heavy concentrations of *Panzer* divisions, roared through the Ardennes, crossing the Meuse on May 13. A hole fifty miles wide was broken in the French fortifications. German troops poured through, storming across France with virtually no opposition. The French leaders were paralyzed, and the Germans reached the sea within seven days. The German line across France cut off escape for the British and French troops to the north in Belgium. When Belgium surrendered on May 28, the Germans had only to tighten the noose to destroy the trapped armies of Britain and France.

A section of the Maginot Line, on which French hopes depended. When it failed, the French were unable to plan an alternative resistance. Their hopes had rested entirely on defensive action.

Camouflage netting concealing a British plane in France.

Above: British and French troops waiting to be picked up from the dunes of Dunkirk. Left: a French volunteer of June 1940 signing up for de Gaulle's Free French to continue resistance against the Germans after the formal surrender.

Dunkirk

The British high command realized the hopelessness of the situation. There was no way they could defeat the oncoming German troops. Their only hope was to rescue their army and live to fight another day. The British and some French troops in Belgium fought their way to the French coastal town of Dunkirk. Relentless attacks of German *Panzers* smashed against the British position. Overhead, the Royal Air Force and the *Luftwaffe* fought for control of the skies.

A call went out for boats, and they came from all along the seacoast of Britain and France. Boats of all sizes—tiny fishing vessels and sightseeing boats, and heavy British battle cruisers—made their way to the coast at Dunkirk. The makeshift flotilla managed to evacuate more than 335,000 soldiers from certain destruction at the hands of the Germans. The British had left behind tons of valuable equipment, but the action at Dunkirk was a tremendous boost to British pride.

The Fall of France

The leadership of France was in disarray, unable to mount an offensive against the Germans. On June 10, Mussolini joined the war on France, hoping that he could take a little French territory as part of the spoils. On June 14, Paris fell and the German flag flew on the Champs Élysées. On June 17, Marshal Pétain, now head of the French state, surrendered.

Hitler had served as a corporal in the First World War and never forgot the humiliation of Germany's defeat. As his revenge, he asked that the surrender of France be signed at Compiègne in the same railcar that had been used for the surrender of Germany in 1918.

By the terms of the surrender, France was divided into two parts. The northern part became an occupied territory under German administration. The southern part would be a separate nation, with its capital at Vichy. Vichy France was led by Fascist Frenchmen who were loyal to Germany. Mussolini received a few square miles of territory in the south of France.

General Charles de Gaulle established a Free French government in Britain, where he coordinated efforts to overthrow the Vichy French and the Germans. Meanwhile, Germany was master of Europe from Poland to the Atlantic. The British prepared hastily, knowing their turn was coming next.

THE BATTLE OF BRITAIN

Hitler now offered peace terms to the British. The British government turned him down, knowing that to abandon Europe to Hitler would be to invite attack later, when Germany was stronger. And indeed, Hitler had drawn up plans for Operation Sea Lion—the invasion of Britain. First, it was necessary to establish supremacy of the skies in order to provide air support for German landing craft.

On July 10, the *Luftwaffe* bombed British ships in the English Channel. The Battle of Britain had begun. It would largely be fought in the air, the first decisive air battle in history. The greatest advantage the British had was a new weapon—radar. This new electronic device enabled them to detect and track enemy aircraft from miles away, even at night.

Field Marshal Hermann Goering, head of the *Luftwaffe,* boasted how quickly Britain would yield to his planes. In the *Luftwaffe*'s early attacks, some of the coastal radar stations were destroyed. But the Germans did not realize their advantage. They felt they were losing too many pilots, and shifted tactics.

In mid-August, the *Luftwaffe* began bombing major industrial targets within Britain. German pilots met with furious resistance from the Royal Air Force (RAF), and suffered heavy losses. Goering switched his attack to the RAF bases, hoping to destroy the British planes on the ground, as he had in Poland. This tactic was starting to work when, on August 25, the RAF bombers staged a raid on Berlin, the German capital.

Goering and Hitler were enraged. They had promised the German people that their enemies would never touch Berlin. The *Luftwaffe* was ordered to concentrate its efforts away from the RAF bases and against cities, particularly London. These attacks, known as the "Blitz," reached a peak on September 15, when the *Luftwaffe* sent more than 1,000 bombers and nearly 700 fighters over London.

Hitler thought the bombings would destroy the spirit of the British, and that they would force the new prime minister, Winston Churchill, to surrender. But the British stood fast. In the words of Churchill, "this was their finest hour." Hitler was forced to postpone Operation Sea Lion. Though bombing of cities in Britain continued for the duration of the war, The Battle of Britain was over.

German Heinkel III bombers over London, like the one shown above, were slower and less maneuverable than the single-seat British Spitfires. In the Battle of Britain, Germany lost twice as many aircraft as Britain.

Right: the British Home Guard were armed civilians who guarded against possible invasions across the English Channel, and hunted down German parachutists. The Home Guard was composed of those too old or too young to fight in the armed forces. Above: civilian volunteers also served as spotters and air-raid wardens. British antiaircraft fire was another effective element in the Battle of Britain. Below: Londoners taking refuge from bombing by sleeping in an underground railway tunnel. The key to Hitler's bombing of cities was his belief that the British people would demand surrender.

Paratroopers and glider-propelled soldiers led the German attack on the island of Crete in May 1941. Parachutists and a plane in flames can be seen in this picture. The world was astonished at their success as Crete fell within a month.

HITLER MOVES EAST

War in the Balkans

Mussolini was looking for an easy target for his military might. On October 28, 1940, Italy invaded Greece from Albania. But the quick victory Mussolini hoped for failed to materialize. The ill-equipped but tough Greek army drove the Italians back. Mussolini sent reinforcements, but by the end of December, the Greeks occupied a quarter of Albania.

Greece asked for help. The British landed troops to protect their air bases in Greece. In April 1941, Hitler invaded both Yugoslavia and Greece. Yugoslavia fell before the *Blitzkrieg* in eleven days, with the Germans taking vicious reprisals against the civilian population. With British help, the Greeks resisted Hitler for a time, but the speed and mobility of the Germans again proved overpowering. In another daring evacuation, 43,000 British soldiers escaped from Greece. Some were transported to the island of Crete; the remainder went to Egypt.

Hitler launched an airborne invasion and drove the British off Crete as well. This was the first major battle fought and won by airborne troops. Bulgaria, Rumania, and Hungary had already yielded to Hitler's demands. Elated by his rapid victories in the Balkans and Eastern Europe, Hitler turned to the biggest target—Russia.

Operation Barbarossa

It was inevitable that the pact between Russia and Germany would fall apart. The Soviet Union, the bastion of world Communism, and Nazi Germany were ideological enemies. The racist ideology of Hitler held that the Russians and other Slavic peoples were *Untermenschen,* or subhumans. For Hitler, the only purpose of the Nonaggression Pact had been to stave off Russia while he used his armies elsewhere. As for Stalin, the pact gave him the time he needed to build up his army.

On June 22, 1941, an immense German force of over 3 million men began the invasion of the Soviet Union. The attack took three broad thrusts—in the north, against Leningrad; in central Russia, against Moscow; and in the south, through the Ukraine. All of these targets were hundreds of miles from the border, but Hitler planned to use *Blitzkrieg* tactics on a vaster scale than ever before.

At first, the Russians were unable to slow the onslaught. Amazingly, the Germans were moving on a front 1,800 miles (2,850 km.) long, with the objective of encircling and destroying the Soviet armies. Hitler thought that a few weeks of fighting would be enough to demonstrate German superiority and break the Russians' will.

On July 3, Stalin issued a call to all Soviet citizens to resist the Germans in every way they could. He instructed the Russian people to follow a "scorched earth" policy—destroy everything of value that the Germans might capture. In the first ten weeks of battle, the German victories were spectacular, and the Soviets suffered more than a million casualties. But the stout resistance of the Soviet army and population cost the Germans 450,000 casualties.

A German gunnery crew in the Soviet Union. Though the Blitzkrieg *tactics were as successful as they had been elsewhere, the great distances involved made a swift victory impossible.*

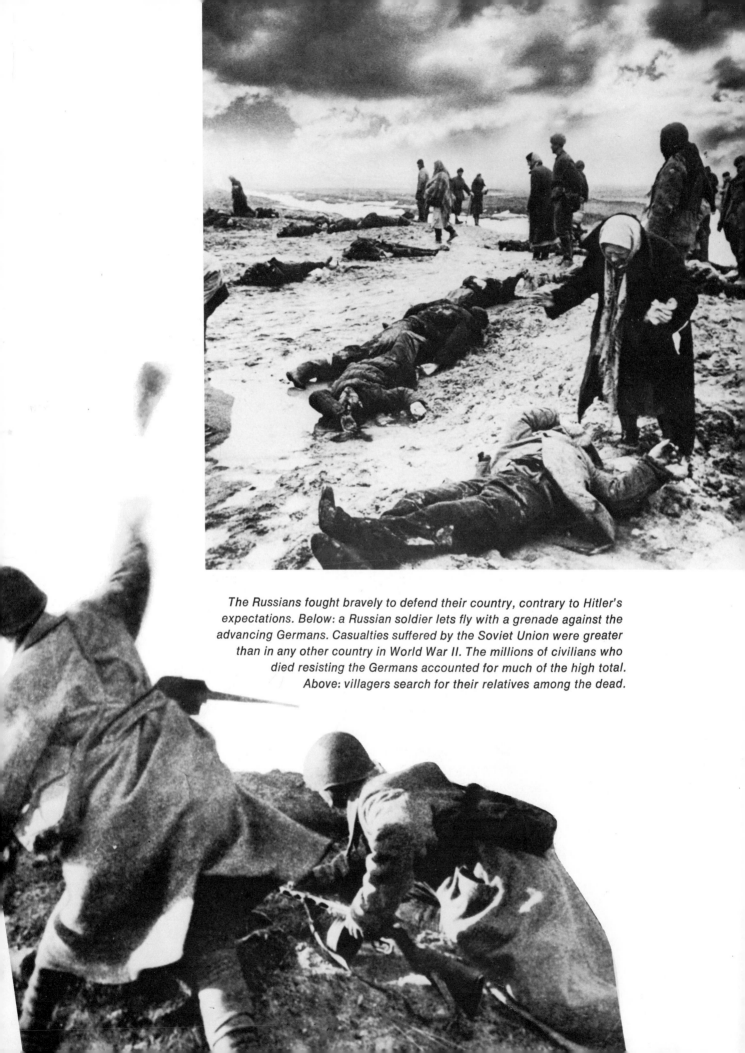

The Russians fought bravely to defend their country, contrary to Hitler's expectations. Below: a Russian soldier lets fly with a grenade against the advancing Germans. Casualties suffered by the Soviet Union were greater than in any other country in World War II. The millions of civilians who died resisting the Germans accounted for much of the high total. Above: villagers search for their relatives among the dead.

In the south, when the Germans marched into the Ukraine, they were hailed as liberators. The Ukrainians had been oppressed by the Communist regime. However, Hitler ordered the same cruel treatment for the Slavic Ukrainians as for all conquered peoples. The support of the rich farming area was thus lost to Hitler, and the Ukrainians united with the other Soviets in resisting Germany.

In the north, with the help of the Finns, the Germans laid siege to the city of Leningrad. The only route to supply the Russian defenders was across Lake Ladoga east of the city. Nonetheless, repeated German attacks failed to crush the city's resistance.

In the central German thrust toward the Russian capital of Moscow, Hitler diverted some troops to capture the city of Kiev. The Kiev defenders surrendered on September 26, but the Germans had lost several weeks of good fighting weather.

The renewed attack on Moscow began in early October. Hitler had always expected a quick victory and made no provision for winter supplies. The Germans' supply lines were over 1,500 miles (2,400 km.) long. And fall rains brought "General Mud" to slow the German tanks.

Panic spread in Moscow as the Germans approached, and the government fled. Stalin stayed in the beleaguered city. On November 7, the anniversary of the Bolshevik revolution, he spoke to the people over the radio. Stalin appealed to loyalty to Mother Russia and pleaded for heroes to arise and once more repel the barbarian invaders. Communist ideology was not stressed.

Marshal Georgi Zhukov, an able commander, was placed in charge of the Russian forces around Moscow. His tactics were to retreat, regrouping his forces until the enemy was exhausted, and then attack. Winter came early in Russia that year. The Germans began to suffer casualties from the weather. On December 6, Zhukov counterattacked. The Germans were driven back, with heavy casualties on both sides. The German general begged Hitler to pull the men back. But Hitler ordered that there be no retreat. Then the worst of the winter set in, slowing the fighting.

At the end of 1941, Hitler reigned supreme from the English Channel to the outskirts of Moscow. Next year, Hitler felt, would bring victory. But the Asian phase of World War II would change the balance. In December 1941, Japan attacked the United States, bringing the U.S. into both the European and Asian wars. The war was now truly global.

THE ASIAN WAR THROUGH JUNE, 1942

THE ROAD TO WAR

Japan after World War I

Since the early 1900s, Japan had been expanding its power and territory in Asia. It annexed Formosa and Korea and acquired influence in Manchuria, a province of China. For entering World War I on the side of the Allies, Japan received the former German territories in the Pacific. Japan had used its role in the war to make demands on China as well. Japan's flag showed a rising sun, and the Japanese believed it was their destiny to be the main power in the Far East.

In the 1920s, Japan suffered from the postwar economic depression. The Japanese government became unstable. Cabinet ministers rose and fell in rapid succession and political assassinations were commonplace. Though the emperor was in name the ruler of Japan, he never interfered with the actual running of the government. In the absence of stable political power, the Japanese military became the effective force in Japan. The policy of the military was to increase Japan's armed forces in order to acquire more power and influence in the Far East.

Japan's giant Asian rival, China, was divided between the national government under Chiang Kai-shek and opposition Communists under Mao Tse-tung. The Chinese were united, however, in their resentment of Japanese exploitation. Boycotts were levied against Japanese goods. Since China was the major market for Japan, continued opposition by the Chinese could have serious consequences.

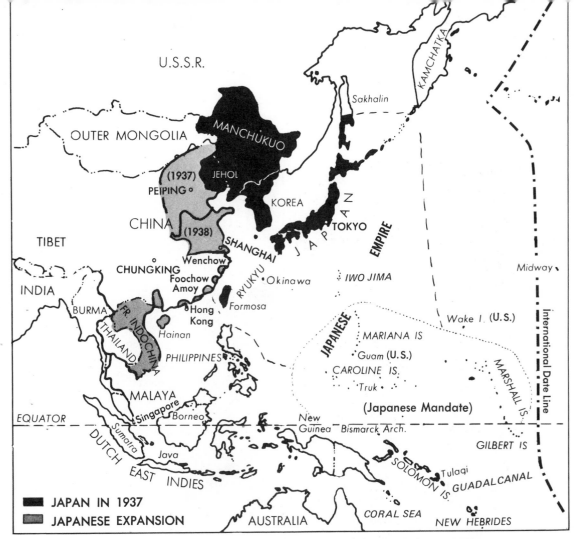

**THE GROWTH OF THE JAPANESE EMPIRE
1937–1941**

Manchurian Incident

In 1931, the friction between China and Japan burst into violence. The Japanese wanted to exploit the Chinese province of Manchuria for its rich natural resources. In September 1931, Japanese agents exploded a bomb on the tracks of the Manchurian railway. Japan blamed the act on Chinese bandits, and sent troops to "restore order." The Japanese troops took over the province and set up a government, which changed the name of the province to Manchukuo. In reality, Manchukuo was a Japanese colony. Two years later, Japanese troops occupied the province of Jehol in northern China and added it to Manchukuo.

The League of Nations condemned the Japanese aggression. Japan responded by pulling out of the League in 1933, the same year the Germans left.

Japanese soldiers in Shanghai in 1937. Six years before, the Japanese seized the city for a short time to force China to drop its trade boycott. Japanese treatment of civilians in 1931 may have accounted for the stout resistance in 1937.

THE WAR IN CHINA

Chinese feeling against Japan hardened after the seizure of Manchuria and Jehol. Other incidents increased the tension. In July 1937, Japanese troops on maneuvers began fighting with Chinese troops guarding the Marco Polo Bridge near Peking. China offered to negotiate the dispute, but the Japanese refused. They moved more forces into northern China and soon captured Peking and Tientsin. Again, the Japanese announced they were seeking to "restore order," but in fact, World War II in Asia had begun.

On August 8, Japanese troops landed in China and began an assault on Shanghai. Chinese resistance was fierce, and the initial attack was thrown back. The Japanese called for reinforcements, and took the city on November 8. But the rest of China was encouraged by the resistance the city had put up.

[30]

From Shanghai, the Japanese made their way up the Yangtze River to capture the Chinese capital of Nanking on December 15. Japanese soldiers sacked the city, looting and terrorizing civilians. News of the "rape of Nanking" reached the outside world, causing more condemnation of the Japanese.

In 1938, the Japanese armies from the south linked up with Japanese forces coming down from Manchukuo. Hankow, the new seat of government, fell on October 25, but Chiang Kai-shek established a new capital farther west in Chungking. More Japanese conquests followed, and the invading armies sealed off the ports through which China was being supplied.

The Japanese had a highly mechanized, well-trained army, equipped with modern weapons. Chinese troops were often disorganized, lacked air and naval support, and were armed with primitive weaponry. But the Chinese did have the advantage of a huge territory and population. They used a "scorched earth" policy against the Japanese, which the Russians would use later against the Germans. Guerrilla troops led by both Chinese Nationalists and Communists continually harassed the Japanese.

By the end of 1939, Japan had cut off all but two of the Chinese supply lines. One ran from Burma to the Chinese city of Kunming. The other came through the port of Haiphong in French Indochina. The Japanese turned their attention to these two objectives, a move which would bring them into conflict with the United States.

Chinese refugees on the Yangtze River. One of the great tragedies of World War II was the displacement of great numbers of people who wandered homelessly through Europe and Asia fleeing the war.

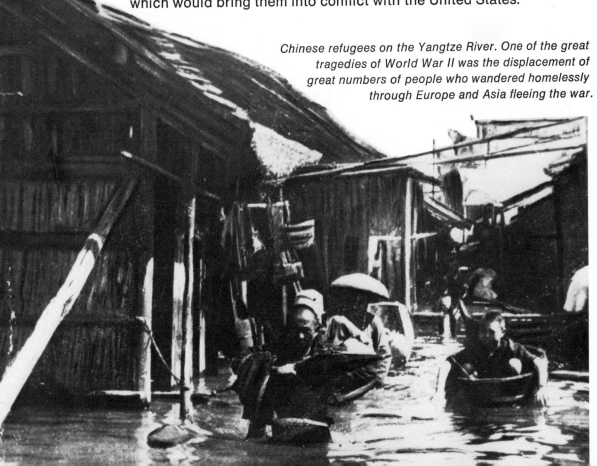

PEARL HARBOR

Prelude

With the fall of France in 1940, the French colony of Indochina was without protection. Japan landed troops in Indochinese ports and closed the railway that ran from Haiphong to Kunming, China. This left the Burma Road as the only supply route to China.

The United States tried to put pressure on Japan to cease its aggression. In 1940, the United States had levied embargoes against aviation fuel, iron, and steel shipments to Japan. But the Japanese continued their pressure on China. For a few months in 1940, they succeeded in closing the Burma Road. After signing the Tripartite Pact with Germany and Italy in September 1940, and a nonaggression pact with the Soviet Union in 1941, Japan moved to further consolidate its control over Indochina. The United States responded by freezing all Japanese assets in America and levying a total embargo on trade with Japan.

The United States was the only nation effectively blocking Japanese control of the European colonies in Southeast Asia. Japan decided that a quick attack on United States forces would give Japan enough time to fortify strategic island positions. By the time the United States prepared a counterattack, the Japanese thought, it would be too costly to try to regain colonies Japan had seized.

Negotiations between the United States and Japan had been going on for some time. Japanese diplomats were still in Washington when the attack came.

Attack

With the rising sun of December 7, 1941, Japanese planes attacked Pearl Harbor. The American fleet was caught completely off guard.

The United States suffered tremendous losses. The Japanese sank eight battleships, three cruisers, and seven smaller ships. Of 394 aircraft on the ground, 108 were totally destroyed and 159 damaged. Americans suffered more than 2,300 dead, 960 missing, and more than 1,100 wounded. The Japanese victory would have been total, except that all three of the American aircraft carriers in the Pacific were not in Pearl Harbor at the time of the attack. Later these carriers were the most important weapons of the naval war.

President Franklin D. Roosevelt convened Congress on December 8 and asked for a declaration of war. Three days later, Italy and Germany declared war on the United States, and the United States reciprocated. The war now stretched all around the world.

[32]

Above: a captured Japanese photograph showing the attack on Pearl Harbor. Japanese planes can be seen on the right of the picture making low-level attacks. The Japanese caption reads: "Two of our Sea Eagles are carrying out a daring low-level attack, reminiscent of the performance of the gods." Below: the American battleships West Virginia and Tennessee after the Japanese attack. Roosevelt called December 7, 1941 "a date that will live in infamy."

JAPAN ADVANCES

On the Mainland

The same day the Japanese attacked Pearl Harbor, they launched an attack on the British colonies of Hong Kong and Malaya. The Japanese military thrusts were fast, furious, and well-planned. By Christmas, Hong Kong was in Japanese hands. The entire British garrison of 12,000 men was killed or captured.

In Malaya, the Japanese attacked on the northern part of the Malayan Peninsula and soon established a beachhead. Two British ships, the *Prince of Wales* and *Repulse,* steamed out of the naval base at Singapore at the opposite end of the peninsula. But the ships had departed without accompanying air cover. Japanese planes arrived from Indochina and sank them.

The British took the Japanese threat too lightly. They assumed that the dense Malayan jungles would hinder the invaders. But the Japanese used the jungles to conceal their movements, which were far swifter and deadlier than the British had believed possible. At the same time, British troops were proving inexperienced and poorly trained. At the end of January, the British withdrew to the sanctuary of the island of Singapore.

Facing page: three Australian soldiers firing an antitank gun against the oncoming Japanese on Singapore. The capture of Singapore gave Japan an important base from which to launch its attacks on the Dutch East Indies and Burma. Left: a section of the Burma Road that ran from India to Kunming, China. Besides navigating such treacherous curves, drivers had to watch out for bombs, attacking troops, road-blocks, and mudslides caused by heavy rains.

Singapore was well defended with coastal fortifications. It was thought to be invulnerable to attack from the sea. No one had foreseen a land invasion from the Malayan jungle. The Japanese bombarded Singapore with artillery and launched waves of bombers against it. In a daring night landing, Japanese soldiers established a foothold on the island. Inch by inch, the Japanese fought their way across the island. Winston Churchill ordered General Arthur Percival, the British commander, to fight to the last man. On February 14, 1942, the Japanese captured the island's water reservoirs. General Percival surrendered the following day. It was a disastrous defeat for the British, and a terrible blow to British pride. In the fighting in Malaya, more than 130,000 British soldiers were taken prisoner, killed, or wounded. Japanese casualties included 3,500 dead and a little more than 6,000 wounded.

At the same time, as part of their well-coordinated war plan, the Japanese invaded Thailand and drove toward Burma and India. By March 7, the Japanese captured Rangoon, the capital of Burma, and by the end of April, they cut the Burma Road, China's last supply link. By now, the Japanese seemed to be threatening to move into the crown jewel of Britain's Asian possessions—India.

[35]

Japanese tanks passing the Filipino Legislature in the streets of Manila. The Japanese thought they would be viewed as liberators by the Filipino people.

In the Pacific

The speed of the Japanese conquests in the Pacific area was just as impressive. The American island possessions of Wake and Guam fell in December 1941. Defending the Dutch East Indies successfully depended on naval support. At the end of February 1942, in the Java Sea, the Japanese navy routed a combined force of American, Dutch, Australian, and British warships. The Dutch East Indian government surrendered on March 9.

A primary objective of the Japanese was the Philippine Islands, a former territory of the United States now given commonwealth status. On the same day as Pearl Harbor, Japanese bombers damaged or destroyed virtually all of the American planes on the ground at Clark Field in the Philippines. Japanese General Masaharu Homma landed 60,000 soldiers in an invasion of the north end of Luzon, the principal Philippine island. They quickly moved south.

General Douglas MacArthur of the United States Army commanded a combined American-Filipino ground force to defend the islands. The Filipinos and Americans had little or no battle experience, and were no match for the seasoned Japanese troops. Japanese bombing of Manila was so heavy that MacArthur abandoned his headquarters there to spare the residents of the city. He moved to Corregidor, an island in Manila Bay, for a last-ditch stand.

Slowly the Japanese drove the island defenders down into the Bataan Peninsula, at the end of which lay Corregidor and the sea. Time and again, MacArthur's forces broke out of traps the Japanese had set. General Homma's forces were depleted, and on February 8, he asked Tokyo for reinforcements.

The Filipinos and Americans knew that the arrival of more Japanese troops would mean the end. There was no way to break the Japanese naval blockade to get supplies or reinforcements to MacArthur. President Roosevelt personally ordered MacArthur to leave the Philippines to command Allied forces elsewhere. Flying to Australia, MacArthur radioed back a message: "I shall return."

With fresh troops, the Japanese moved inexorably south. On April 9, 40,000 Americans and Filipinos on Bataan surrendered. The prisoners were forced to march through the steaming jungle to prisons in Manila. Hundreds died on the "Bataan Death March," and thousands more died in the filthy prisons. On May 6, after bloody fighting, the last defenders on the island of Corregidor fell.

Between January and April, the Japanese had extended their area of influence by seizing the Gilbert and Admiralty Islands. They also established bases in New Guinea from which they could bomb Australia. After the fall of Corregidor, the Japanese controlled almost all the important islands of the Pacific west of Midway to the Philippines, plus large areas on the mainland of Asia. Their plan had worked. Japan now controlled all the resources it yearned for.

American soldiers and sailors surrendering on Corregidor. One reason the Japanese treated prisoners cruelly was that they thought it cowardly to surrender.

JAPAN CHECKED

The Doolittle Raid
A squadron of American bombers led by Colonel James Doolittle unexpectedly bombed Tokyo on April 18, 1942. The Doolittle raid stunned the Japanese, who were feeling confident about their quick and complete victories. The Japanese, like the Germans, had told their people that the capital would never be bombed. Aside from the boost in American morale it provided, the raid made the Japanese keep a number of fighter planes at home to defend against attacks.

The Battle of the Coral Sea
Through the secret decoding of Japanese messages, called Project MAGIC, the Americans learned of the next steps in the Japanese plan. Tulagi in the Solomon Islands and Port Moresby on New Guinea were the new targets. The Americans sent the only two available aircraft carriers, the *Yorktown* and the *Lexington,* to the Coral Sea to counter the Japanese attacks.

In the five-day battle that resulted from the confrontation, none of the opposing ships came within sight of each other. The battle was fought by carrier-based planes sent against the opposing fleets. The Japanese carrier *Shokaku* was severely damaged, and the Japanese lost a large number of planes. Both American carriers were damaged, the *Lexington* so badly that she had to be scuttled. The invasion of Port Moresby was called off.

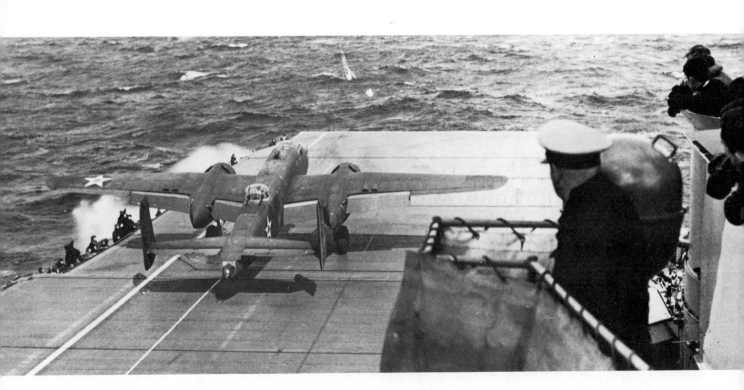

Facing page: one of Colonel James Doolittle's planes taking off from the deck of the U.S.S. Hornet. One of the things that amazed the Japanese about the raid was that they could not discover where the planes had come from. Left: a Japanese destroyer hit by an American torpedo at the Battle of Midway, as seen through the periscope of an American submarine.

Midway

The Japanese now went after the American island of Midway, a key in the defense of the Pacific. Admiral Isoroku Yamamoto, commander of the Japanese fleet, sent a diversionary attack to the Aleutian Islands near Alaska. Since the Americans were still reading the Japanese messages, Admiral Chester Nimitz reinforced Midway's defending forces and prepared a fleet of twenty-nine major ships and nineteen submarines against the oncoming attack.

On June 4, 1942, Japanese bombers with their Zero fighter-escort planes broke through the defenders at Midway. The Zeros protected the Japanese carriers so well that not a single American plane could counterattack. The next day, the opposing naval forces threw their full strength at each other. Plane after American plane was shot down by the Japanese. No torpedo-carrying planes or fighters could get through to the Japanese carriers.

But then American dive bombers were sent to take up the fierce attack. In a stunning reversal, the dive bombers sank or destroyed four Japanese carriers. The battle raged for three days and nights till Yamamoto ordered a withdrawal. His forces had suffered the greatest naval defeat in Japanese history. The Japanese lost 275 planes and more than 4,800 men, including some of their most experienced pilots. The Japanese would never be on the offensive again. Midway had turned the tide.

THE OTHER WAR

THE POLITICS OF WAR

The Allies

Churchill, Roosevelt, and Stalin, the heads of the principal Allied nations, were known as the "Big Three." Although they had different and sometimes conflicting goals, their ability to cooperate and coordinate strategy was crucial to the Allied victory.

From the time Churchill became Prime Minister, he kept close ties to Roosevelt. The two met on a warship in Placentia Bay in Newfoundland, Canada in the summer of 1941 to draw up the Atlantic Charter, a statement of conditions that should prevail in a postwar world. In December 1941, Roosevelt and Churchill again met, this time in Washington, D.C., and determined that the primary thrust of the war would be to defeat Hitler. After that, the concentration would be on Japan. At a third meeting, in 1943 at Casablanca, Roosevelt declared the Allies' aim was to secure "unconditional surrender."

The "Big Three": Stalin, Roosevelt, and Churchill meet face-to-face for the first time at Teheran. Besides planning strategy against the Axis, each of the three had his own plans for a postwar world.

Stalin was at times a difficult ally. Roosevelt and Churchill were sending supplies to the Soviet Union, but Stalin demanded more. From the start, he insisted that the Allies open a "second front" by invading France and drawing Hitler's troops away from the Russian front. When the invasion was delayed, or when shipments of supplies slowed because of German submarine attacks, Stalin would accept no excuses. At the Teheran Conference in November 1943, the Allies finally agreed to invade France the following year, and Stalin was placated for a time.

The Axis

By contrast, the Axis nations did not coordinate their strategy. Although Germany and Italy joined Japan in declaring war on the United States, they never assisted Japan in the fighting in Asia. Because Japan had an alliance with the Soviet Union, it never responded to Hitler's pleas to make war on Russia. A second front against Russia would have strained Stalin's capacity to resist the Germans, but Japan respected their treaty until the last days of the war.

In Europe, Hitler reigned supreme. Mussolini was never more than a junior partner in the alliance, and in the end he was less than that. His aggressive postures in the Balkans and North Africa got him into difficulties. Hitler had to expend manpower, material, and time to bail him out.

Italian, German, and Japanese flags waved together on the main street of Tokyo in 1937 to commemorate the Anti-Comintern Pact, which brought the three nations together.

Left: Japanese propaganda poster intended for the Philippines. The Philippines remained loyal to the U.S. even after Japanese capture of the islands. Above: the "New Order" at work. A group of Nazi policemen in Berlin arresting a German Jew who argues in vain against his deportation. One Jew who fled Hitler's Germany was Albert Einstein, who played a key role in the development of America's atomic bomb.

Somewhere in China, resistance workers make bombs for use against the Japanese invaders.

OCCUPIED COUNTRIES

The New Order in Europe

In conquered Europe, Hitler planned to establish what he called "The New Order." Portrayed as a society of culture and refinement, what the New Order actually became was a Europe whose resources and people were exploited for the needs of the German "supermen." The SS, a Nazi elite corps, headed by Heinrich Himmler, was ruthless in its use of terror to subdue the "inferior," conquered peoples. The ultimate fate of the Slavs and Jews under Nazism was to be extermination, but in the meantime they were used as slave workers and as material for "scientific" experiments. All who protested, German or non-German, were to suffer the same fate.

The Greater East Asia Co-prosperity Sphere

The Japanese name for the empire they hoped to establish in the Far East and Pacific was the Greater East Asia Co-prosperity Sphere. This was to be a peaceful confederation of Asian peoples under the leadership of the Japanese. The Japanese were to be the liberators who would help the Asiatic peoples throw off their colonial chains. The Japanese, in fact, were often welcomed as liberators. But when it became clear that Japan intended to exploit the natural resources and people of Asia in much the same way as Europeans had, the natives turned against the Japanese. China had learned its lesson very early, in Manchuria, and the one unifying idea of the Chinese was to throw out the invaders. Like Hitler's New Order, the Greater East Asia Co-prosperity Sphere was good only for Japan.

Resistance Movements

Native populations in all occupied countries resisted their conquerers with organized and individual activities. In some countries, such as France, the resistance was a formal organization that sometimes received its orders over the radio from a distant city where the ousted government still operated. But the resistance included any spur-of-the-moment act of sabotage, sometimes including violence against occupying soldiers. In Paris, it was said, no German was safe alone. In other countries, work stoppages and industrial espionage helped the Allied cause. Norwegian resistance fighters sabotaged the shipment of Hitler's only source of "heavy water," a vital necessity for building an atomic bomb. In countries such as the Soviet Union and China, civilians continually harassed the German

[43]

The fate of a French resistance fighter.
The dangers of resisting were such that
most people in occupied Europe found it
easier just to go on about their daily lives.

and Japanese troops who were actively fighting. Citizens of occupied countries often fled to neutral or Allied countries, where they formed military units that fought under Allied command.

Captured resistance fighters were subjected to torture and death. Sometimes even nonresisting people were brutalized. The town of Lidice, in Czechoslovakia, was wiped out by Hitler in retaliation for the assassination of Reinhold Heydrich, a high-ranking Nazi.

Not all inhabitants of occupied countries resisted. Some were active collaborators with the Nazis. And many did whatever they felt necessary to survive.

Communists supported the resistance in all occupied countries. Some Communist resistance leaders became leaders of their countries after the war. Tito of Yugoslavia, Mao Tse-tung of China, and Ho Chi Minh of Vietnam were among these.

THE HOME FRONT

Importance of the War at Home

The contributions of civilians to the war effort on the home-front played a vital role in the Allied and Axis nations. Industry, science, and agriculture were the backup systems of modern warfare. The war itself was fought to secure control of the supplies necessary to make war. Colossal amounts of war material came pouring from the factories and mines as each country placed its production facilities on a wartime basis. Coordinated economic planning put industry at the service of the war effort. In Germany, Albert Speer was the able planner who guided the industrial production, but his ability always took a backseat to Hitler's brainstorms. Hitler preferred spectacular breakthroughs to the steady economic and scientific production that in the end won the war for the Allies.

Huge sums of money were devoted to scientific research for the war. There were spectacular developments such as radar, rockets, and finally the atomic bomb. Yet the smallest mechanical and technological developments were all vital to the difference between victory and defeat. Engines that could operate efficiently in extremes of cold or heat, new types of textiles to clothe soldiers properly, more accurate bombsights, and countless other developments were part of the scientific contribution to the war. Medical research, resulting in such wonder drugs as penicillin, had a particular importance.

*The British Women's Land Army in action.
Typists, clerks, and sales personnel from the
city help out during the harvest season.*

American women service personnel were forbidden to engage in combat. But this woman Marine was trained as an aerial photographer to free a male Marine for battle duty.

Producing enough food to keep the combatants supplied was critical. Work on farms was the contribution of women and those too young or too old to fight.

More than ever before, women played a role in warfare. In countries on a full war economy, women took men's places in factories, laboratories, and sometimes on the firing line as well.

The dangers of the war were brought home too. Air power could transport the war to any spot on the globe. Even in the United States, which was never bombed, blackouts became a part of daily life.

Propaganda reached new heights of sophistication as technology was used in new ways to build morale at home and break the enemy's spirit. Radios could receive the broadcasts of friends and foes alike. Allied troops often listened to Axis Sally and Tokyo Rose play the latest in New York dance music and then ask the question, "Who's your girl out with tonight, G.I.?"

The Arsenal of Democracy

The Allies' greatest economic asset was the industrial strength of the United States. The U.S. became known as "the arsenal of democracy."

American participation in the war began in 1941 with Roosevelt's "Lend-Lease," in which he authorized shipments of war material to Britain, China, and later, the Soviet Union.

Because it was never bombed, the United States turned out a phenomenal amount of goods—enough not only to keep its own troops supplied, but to support the besieged populations of China, Russia, Britain, and other countries fighting invaders and bombers on their own soil. From about 1943, the Nazis and the Japanese suffered crippling losses of planes, ships, and equipment that they could not replace. But the arsenal of democracy was operating at full strength, keeping the Allied forces fully equipped.

An ugly persecution marred the American war effort. Japanese-Americans living on the west coast of the United States were interned and placed in guarded camps. Fear of "disloyalty" was the reason for this action, though there had never been any incident to show that the Japanese-Americans were disloyal. In fact, Japanese-American troops fought bravely for the Allied cause. Moreover, German-Americans and Italian-Americans were never interned.

The arsenal of democracy turns out another transport ship. The sign indicates that the entire ship was completed in just ten working days. The spirit of workers during the war was one of enthusiasm, as each struggled to surpass the factory's quota.

THE EUROPEAN WAR 1942–1944

THE WAR IN NORTH AFRICA

The Italian Campaign

With the Battle of Britain raging, Mussolini thought he might have a chance to take the British-dominated kingdom of Egypt. The Italian colony of Libya lay on Egypt's western border, and Mussolini prepared to launch an attack from there. In September 1940, Italian troops moved into Egypt to Sidi Barrani, where they stopped to prepare the main attack. The commander of British Middle East forces, General Archibald Wavell, became aware of the Italian preparations. In December, he decided to launch a surprise attack. The Italians were caught unawares and imagined that the British forces must be far superior in numbers than they actually were. The British chased the Italians clear across Libya to Benghazi, in a complete rout. By early February 1941, the British killed or wounded more than 10,000 Italians and took more than 130,000 prisoners. Total British casualties were less than 2,000.

Italian soldiers during the early fighting in North Africa. Part of the problem with the Italians was their timid commander, Marshal Rodolfo Graziani, who had to be urged onward every time he advanced a few miles.

*General Rommel
in North Africa.*

Rommel to the Rescue

Hitler was alarmed by the failure of the Italians, and sent one of his best young commanders, General Erwin Rommel, to Africa in early 1941. With a crack body of German troops called the *Afrika Korps,* Rommel took command of a new Italian army. They fought with great courage and skill under Rommel's direction.

Rommel hit the British with a devastating attack that pushed them back to the Egyptian border. The British held one position inside Libya, at Tobruk, behind Rommel's lines. For the rest of the year the fighting was a seesaw affair, as the British applied pressure from Tobruk while attacking from the Egyptian side as well.

This section of the desert was particularly barren and unpopulated. It became a testing ground for the military tactics of the two sides. The road along the coast, which both armies used, turns in a huge curve from Tobruk to Benghazi. Attackers sent their tanks to engage the enemy on the road, while sending another force across the desert to catch the enemy from behind. The only effective countermeasure was to retreat fast enough to keep from being encircled. Both sides advanced back and forth through 1941 in these actions, called by the troops "The Benghazi Handicaps," because they were like horse races.

Finally in a gigantic battle of tanks, during which the British alone lost 835 of their 900 tanks, Rommel took Tobruk in June 1942. Seizing the advantage he drove the British back to El Alamein.

[49]

El Alamein

Rommel's advance threatened Egypt and the vital Suez Canal. Britain and the United States rushed reinforcements and supplies to the Allied defenders. Rommel realized that the longer he waited, the greater numerical advantage the other side would have. He tried for a victory that would knock out the Allies in North Africa for good.

El Alamein was a good spot for the British to defend. Directly to the south was the Qattara Depression—a section of the desert through which tanks and large numbers of troops could not travel. Rommel could not use his tactics of encirclement.

Rommel attacked on August 31. The opposing Allied forces were led by a British commander, General Bernard Montgomery. Repeatedly, the *Afrika Korps* attempted a breakthrough, but the Allies pushed them back. Hitler could no longer send supplies in sufficient quantity to Rommel, and the attack lost its strength. Rommel prepared to pull back to a defensive position, but Hitler sent orders once again that there was to be no retreat.

On October 23, Montgomery counterattacked. The British now had superior strength in the air and on the ground. Rommel was short of tanks and fuel, and began to give ground. He slowed the British advance with every tactic he knew, carefully avoiding the many traps that Montgomery set. Aided by Free French soldiers Montgomery drove the Germans back to Tripoli, the capital of Libya. Rommel and his men escaped to Tunisia, where they established a defensive position that held off the British and French.

Australian troops advancing under fire in North Africa. The British garrison in Egypt was composed of troops from Australia, Canada, South Africa, New Zealand, and India.

Mediterranean Area and Africa

Operation TORCH

In November 1942, American and British troops under the command of American General Dwight Eisenhower landed in French Morocco and Algeria in northwest Africa. The invasion was known as Operation TORCH. After subduing the Vichy French defenders, who were allies of the Germans, the Americans and British established a position to the rear of Rommel's forces.

By this time, Hitler realized that Allied bases in northern Africa could be used to launch air and sea attacks on southern Europe. He sent more reinforcements to the *Afrika Korps.* Rommel realized that Eisenhower's troops were inexperienced and disorganized. He prepared a thrust to break through the Allies advancing from the west. Launching a surprise attack, Rommel cut through the Allied forces and advanced toward the Kasserine Pass in western Tunisia. If he had broken through the pass, he would have been within reach of the main supply and communications headquarters for the Allies in Tunisia. But the Allies halted Rommel at the Kasserine Pass.

Now the Germans were caught in a vise, with Montgomery on one side and Eisenhower on the other. Slowly the Germans retreated to Bizerte and Tunis. Hitler called for more attacks, though the *Afrika Korps* had no resources for an attack. Hitler ordered no evacuation, no retreat, no surrender. As a result, more than 275,000 Axis prisoners were taken by the Allies. Some of the most skilled soldiers of the German army were among the prisoners and out of the way for good.

THE WAR IN RUSSIA

The German Offensive

During the winter of 1941, the Germans fortified the Russian cities that they held all along the two-thousand-mile (3,200-km.) front. Using any means they could, the Germans sought shelter from the cold, while the Russian winter counteroffensive petered out. By the spring both armies had been reinforced. Hitler was planning two further Russian offensives for the summer of 1942. Both were to be carried out in the southern sphere of operations.

The first offensive was the capture of Sevastopol in the Crimea. Much of the rest of the Crimean peninsula had been taken by the Germans during 1941. With the fall of Sevastopol, Germany would have control of the Black Sea. They would then be within striking distance of the Russian oil fields. The attack was launched on June 7, 1942. After a fierce struggle lasting four weeks, the city of Sevastopol fell early in July.

Now the second offensive had begun. The Germans planned to move eastward on an enormous front to capture the city of Stalingrad on the Volga in the north and Baku, which commanded the Caucasus oil fields in the south. Capture of the fields would supply the Germans with badly needed oil, and shut off the Russian supply. The Caucasus region also contained the last remaining major agricultural area within the Soviet Union. Without its products, the Soviets would face mass starvation.

The gigantic offensive was launched June 28. By now, the German line throughout the Soviet Union was nearly 3,000 miles (4,800 km.) long. Resistance by Russians behind the German lines was fierce, continuous, and damaging.

The Germans moved speedily in the first month of the offensive, covering over 300 miles (480 km.). But as the lines neared the cities of Baku and Stalingrad, the attack slowed. The Germans didn't have sufficient troop strength to take both places.

Stalingrad

Hitler was furious at the delay. He ordered an immediate assault on Stalingrad, just as Stalin himself decided to defend the city to the end. With both sides devoting great resources of men and equipment to the battle, Stalingrad became a crucial turning point in the war.

On September 13, German troops broke into Stalingrad. Meeting heavy resistance, the Germans fought their way forward. Fighting raged over each building, each city block, from the middle of Sep-

Right: a German tank rolls over Russian soldiers in the trench below. After it passes, they will destroy it with their grenades. Below: his artillery weapon smashed, his comrades dead, a German soldier awaits capture by the Russians.

tember, all through October and into November. The Germans controlled over three-fourths of the city, but the Russians fought on.

On November 19, the Soviets brought up reserves outside the city for a counterattack. Under Marshal Zhukov, they hit the German positions. After four days of fighting, Zhukov closed an enormous ring around the German armies. The trap had been sprung.

General Friedrich von Paulus, commander of the 300,000 Germans in the city and outskirts, wanted to fight his way out of the trap. Hitler saw this as a cowardly retreat, and ordered him to hold his position. There was little or no shelter from the winter cold in the ravaged city. Lack of food and supplies further weakened the German troops. Finally, on January 31, 1943, General von Paulus gave up the fight. All German resistance ended on February 2. There were only 90,000 starving Germans left. Hitler's *Wehrmacht* had suffered a colossal defeat.

Malnutrition was common within the beleagured city of Leningrad. This man holds his extra ration of bread allotted to him because he is suffering from malnutrition.

Fighting inside Stalingrad in what once was a street. The devastation of the city was almost complete.

With the defeats at El Alamein and Stalingrad, the myth of Nazi invincibility died. The German victories were over. In the spring of 1943, the Russians turned the tide and began advancing westward.

Rather than falling back and allowing time to regroup, Hitler ordered another attack in the summer of 1943. This time the target was the Russian position around the city of Kursk. But Zhukov was there again, preparing a strong defensive position, and the German attack failed. The Germans reeled backward, leaving behind thousands of irreplaceable soldiers and their valuable equipment.

From now on, the Russian strategy was to press steadily against one part of the German line until German reinforcements arrived from another part of the front. Then the Russian attack would shift to a weaker spot. By the end of March 1944, the Ukraine farming area was again in Soviet hands. The Russians liberated Sevastopol on May 9. It was only a matter of time until Russian soil would be free of Germans. But the Russians were headed for Berlin.

The Siege of Leningrad

Leningrad had been under siege by the Germans since the latter part of 1941. The Germans surrounded the city on three sides. Only a trickle of food and supplies was getting across Lake Ladoga to the city. Many starved as the siege continued for months, then years.

After the Soviets were successful against the Germans on other fronts, Stalin gave orders for the Red Army to break the siege. On January 15, 1944, the Russians launched a surprise attack on the German forces. Within two weeks, the Germans had fallen back 100 miles (160 km.). The city had survived.

Below: a convoy of merchant ships crossing the Atlantic together for safety. The aircraft whose wing can be seen in the right-hand corner was part of the protective escort. Right: sailors of the North Atlantic faced dangers not only from enemy ships and subs but also from bitter winter cold and storms.

THE WAR AT SEA

The Battle of the Atlantic

Control of the seas was important for supplying allies, moving and landing troops, and disrupting the naval operations of enemies. In the First World War, the convoy system had been developed to bring merchant ships safely through hostile waters. In World War II, the convoys became larger to accommodate the enormous amounts of supplies that flowed from the United States to its allies. The German U-boats, as they had been in the earlier war, were a constant threat to shipping.

The naval war began the first day of the war when a British ship, the *Athenia,* was torpedoed and sunk by a German U-boat. Though the German submarine fleet was small, its technology had advanced since the British last encountered it. The Germans were equipped to lay magnetic mines in the shipping lanes. To counter these mines, the British had to degauss (demagnetize) their merchant ships before sailing.

The British also lacked long-range escort ships to protect the convoys. Usually, the escorts only accompanied the convoys 200 miles (320 km.) west of the Irish coast. With their victories in western Europe in 1940, the Germans were able to establish submarine bases on the Atlantic coast from France to Norway. From these, submarines could venture far out into the Atlantic and sink ships after their escorts had left them. The British had to double the range of the escorts.

Admiral Karl Doenitz, the commander of the German U-boats, began to build up his fleet. When it was discovered that British sonar detectors could not "see" ships on the surface, Doenitz ordered submarines to surface before attacking.

Doenitz came up with another effective tactic, that of the "wolf pack." The German submarines would fan out in a long line, searching for enemy ships. When one was found, the other submarines would be radioed its position, and all would swoop down on it. This was particularly effective against lightly guarded convoys.

By April of 1941, Admiral Doenitz's wolf packs had cut back Allied shipping by one-half. In the entire war, more than 32,000 British merchant seamen died, out of a total of 145,000 who served. This was a higher casualty rate than for any other branch of the service. In 1941, the wolf packs were so successful that Britain was in danger of being starved out of the war.

Only the assistance of the United States kept the British supplied. Even though the United States was not officially in the war till December 1941, it was acting as an ally of Britain earlier in the year. German and American ships exchanged occasional fire throughout 1941. After the German declaration of war on the United States, the U-boats eagerly pounced on American merchant ships, even in the coastal waters of the United States.

March of 1943 was the high point of the German naval warfare. The U-boats sank forty-three Allied merchant ships in the North Atlantic in the first twenty days of the month. But between mid-May and September of that year, not a single Allied ship was lost in the Atlantic. The difference was the arrival of more sophisticated radar. Unlike the sonar, the new radar sets could detect surface ships. Now Allied aircraft, equipped with radar, patrolled the Atlantic, bombing German subs. The submarines now had a serious handicap in that they had to surface regularly to take air aboard for the crew and to permit their diesel engines to recharge the batteries that powered the ship under water.

Doenitz told Hitler that the U-boat campaign would have to be called off. Hitler promised new weapons. The first of these was a homing torpedo, which used a listening device to "home in" on the propeller of a merchant ship. The homing torpedoes were effective until the Allies countered them with "foxers." A foxer was towed on a line far behind the ship. It made a noise louder than the propeller, and the homing torpedoes steered harmlessly for it.

Coastguardsmen scrape oil from a seaman who was rescued after his ship had been sunk off North Africa.

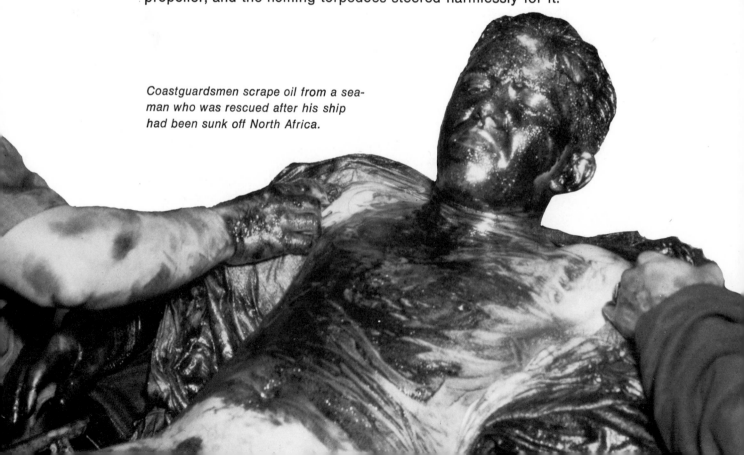

"Loose lips sink ships" was another slogan that reflected the Allies' fear that spies could relay valuable shipping information to the enemy.

At last the Germans developed a snorkel device that eliminated the need for U-boats to surface and expose themselves to radar-guided bombers. But by this time, the United States was turning out ships too fast for the U-boat fleet to make a significant difference. The Battle of the Atlantic was a victory for the Allies.

Conventional Naval Warfare

There were only isolated examples of conventional naval warfare in the war. In December 1939, the British used superior tactics to defeat the German battleship *Graf Spee* with three smaller ships. The captain of the *Graf Spee* scuttled his ship rather than surrender.

In the spring of 1941, the giant battleship *Bismarck,* together with the *Prinz Eugen,* were sinking Allied merchant vessels in the North Atlantic. The *Bismarck* was so heavily plated that it was thought to be unsinkable. However, a combined air and naval attack by British forces sent it to the bottom after a fierce fight. After that, Hitler's naval warfare was left to the U-boats.

From the standpoint of naval tactics, one of the most important battles of the western seas was on November 11, 1940. The Italian fleet was knocked out of the war at Taranto, Italy, by planes from the British aircraft carrier *Illustrious.* Only two British planes were lost, and the *Illustrious* was never in danger. This was the first instance in warfare of effective use of carrier-based planes. Admiral Yamamoto in Tokyo was much impressed by news accounts of the battle. He would use the same tactics later against the Americans in the Pacific, and so revolutionize modern naval warfare.

[59]

Fighter planes, like this P-51, had to be sleek and easily maneuverable and at the same time had to carry enough fuel to accompany the long-range bombers on their missions.

THE AIR WAR

Troop support by aircraft in the First World War was usually limited to scouting. The few bombing raids by plane and Zeppelin were of little consequence to the outcome of the war. But in World War II, it was clear from the start that neither side could win the war without air superiority. The plane was the crucial element of the war whether in the great sea battles, which were fought between aircraft carriers and submarine attackers, or in the *blitzkrieg* warfare that required air support, or in the amphibious invasions that needed protection from the fighters and bombers overhead. Air warfare was used to soften up troop emplacements, to intimidate enemy populations, and to destroy supplies, communications, and industries.

When the United States joined the war, it had differing views from its British allies on the types of bombings that they wanted against Germany. The British wanted night bombing against general targets. The Americans were more concerned with precision bombing against selected industrial targets. Precision bombing was best done in the daytime, when more effective antiaircraft fire resulted in greater losses. General bombing, however, could be done at night with greater safety for the pilots. In the end, both types were used.

The Cologne, Dresden, and Hamburg bombings were devastating attacks on German cities. The war was being brought home to the Germans in hopes of breaking their spirit, but it can be argued that attacks on industrial targets were more effective.

Bombing attacks had to be supported by long-range fighters. The fighter pilots carried combat into the air, and gradually the Allies won out over the *Luftwaffe.*

The American factories pouring out new planes for attack were never touched by the enemy. Nor were Russian factories that had been moved to the Urals, out of reach of the longest-range German bombers. In the end, the industrial might of the Allies won the battle. Skilled German pilots were also difficult to replace, and by the end of the war, the Germans were using boys in gliders.

Left: an American bomber swoops low over an oil refinery at Ploesti, in German-controlled Rumania. Low approaches were more dangerous to pilots, but were necessary for effective pin-point bombing. Below: a search-light in Berlin probes the night sky for signs of Allied bombers. With the limited radar the Germans had, it was difficult to shoot enemy planes at night.

THE LIBERATION OF EUROPE

CONQUEST OF ITALY

Sicily

With the Germans defeated in North Africa, the Allies could cross the Mediterranean to Italy. The first objective was the island of Sicily, a base for German air power and submarines. On July 10, 1943, American and British forces landed on the south and east coasts of the island. After repelling a German *Panzer*-led counter-attack, they moved swiftly across the island. On July 22, Palermo, the capital of Sicily, fell to the Allies. The Germans began an orderly withdrawal across the Strait of Messina, and by August 17, the German forces had escaped safely to the mainland.

Right: Allied troops received as liberators in the streets of Palermo. Facing page: the ruins of Monte Cassino. Some Allied commanders became convinced that the monastery was being used as an observation post by the Germans and ordered its destruction. After the war, it was shown that the monks had not permitted the Germans to use the monastery before the bombing.

Meanwhile, Mussolini's popularity among the Italians had been dwindling rapidly. Wartime conditions in Italy were hard, and the Italians were disillusioned with Mussolini's empty dream of empire. On July 25, 1943, Mussolini was overthrown and imprisoned. Marshal Pietro Badoglio formed a new government, which began secret peace negotiations with the Allies. But the Germans rescued Mussolini and brought him to northern Italy, where he set up a new government that was protected by German troops.

Southern Italy

Allied troops crossed the Strait of Messina on September 3, 1943 and began the invasion of the Italian mainland. On September 8, Badoglio's government formally surrendered. The Italian navy was sent to join the Allied fleet in Malta. But the *Luftwaffe* attacked the fleet at sea and partially destroyed it. German soldiers brushed aside Italian resistance and took over the government at Rome. In southern Italy, the Germans disarmed Italian troops to prevent them from joining the Allies. In a few hours, Italy had gone from being an ally of Germany to an occupied country.

More Allied troops landed farther up the coast, at Salerno. The Germans had anticipated this move. German counterattacks, planned in advance, nearly drove the Allies back into the sea. They held on grimly, pouring reinforcements into their tiny beachhead. The tide turned when the Germans ran out of reinforcements and Allied forces moved up from the Strait of Messina.

[63]

Left: an American of Japanese descent sighting his rifle in Italy. The all-Japanese–American 100th Infantry Battalion was the most heavily decorated American unit in the war. Above: Black Americans, like the Japanese-Americans, served in segregated units during the war. These infantrymen are crossing the Arno River preparatory to storming German positions.

German troops taken prisoner by the Americans fighting in Italy are marched to a holding area.

Advancing North

Italy is a mountainous country with many rivers. This terrain slowed the advance of the Allied troops. In October, the Germans began a retreat to their defensive "Winter Line." They cleverly picked areas in which the terrain strengthened the fortifications. The Allies were unable to advance.

By this time, Allied plans for the invasion of western Europe required the removal of seasoned troops from Italy. They were replaced by green soldiers fresh from training camps. The Allies debated whether these troops should be used only to hold the line in Italy, or to try to continue advancing north. The decision was made to press the attack against the Germans in Italy. This would require Hitler to squander his precious reinforcements, taking them from western Europe.

The Allies made an amphibious landing at Anzio, on the other side of the Winter Line, in January of 1944. But the Germans moved reinforcements up quickly, and the Allied troops could not break out for a thrust at the Winter Line.

The town of Cassino occupied a strategic position on the Winter Line. Time after time Allied attacks from the south were thrown back from the strongly fortified German positions. The ancient monastery of Monte Cassino stood on a mountain overlooking the battle area. Allied planes bombed and destroyed the monastery in February. But the Germans moved into the ruins and used the position to throw back the allies once again. Not until May 18 did Monte Cassino fall to Polish troops who had made their way up the mountain under heavy fire.

When reinforcements finally arrived at the Anzio beachhead, the Allies broke out. The Winter Line began to crumble. Allied troops marched triumphantly into Rome on June 4, liberating the city from German rule. But the German forces retreated and escaped destruction. In the mountains of northern Italy, they constructed another defensive position called the Gothic Line. From here, they were able to hold off the Allies until the end of April 1945, a week before Berlin itself fell.

In April 1945, as the Allies were breaking through the Gothic Line, Mussolini tried to flee with the retreating Germans. He was captured by Italian partisan troops and executed on April 28. The Germans surrendered on April 29.

The scene at the Normandy beachhead. LSTs and troop transports disgorge an endless stream of reinforcements.

D-DAY

Just as western Europe waited for the Nazi attacks in 1940, the Germans now waited for the Allied assault on Fortress Europe. Churchill and Roosevelt agreed on General Eisenhower as commander of Operation Overlord, as the invasion plan was called. His orders were to enter Europe, aiming at the heart of Germany.

Planning for the invasion was on a vast scale, with every detail accounted for. Throughout 1943, southern England was turned into a military camp. A pipeline was constructed across the English Channel to transport the oil needed to supply the troops. Special landing craft were constructed to handle the huge invasion force. All of this planning had to be done in secrecy. The Germans reinforced the ports along the French coast in preparation for the coming invasion. Seeing these preparations, the Allies decided to surprise the Germans by picking an invasion site on the Normandy coast that did not have a good port. They devised artificial docking facilities known as "mulberries." Meanwhile, the Germans laid mines, underwater obstacles, and steel and concrete obstructions. Hitler was constructing what was known as the Atlantic Wall.

The date for Operation Overlord was set for the first week of June 1944, with the actual invasion day (D-Day) dependent on the weather. The Allies had about one million men ready to invade, with another million backing them up with supplies, medical care, and transport. Naval and air support troops numbered nearly another million. It was to be the largest amphibious invasion in history.

The Allies knew that the Germans would be swift and strong with their counterattack. It was necessary to get as many men ashore as fast as possible. Bomber targets shifted from German cities to troops and railways in France. This was done in order to soften up the opposition and disrupt troop movements. They were helped by resistance fighters who destroyed radar stations. Paratroopers would land a few hours before the invasion to confuse the Germans and help establish a defensive perimeter. The closest French port to the English coast was at Calais, and the Allies made several false moves toward Calais to convince the Germans that the intended attack site was there.

On June 6, the weather was right and Eisenhower gave the order to begin. At 2:00 A.M. the paratroopers began to land on the beaches of Normandy. Planes bombed the attack site fortifications. At 6:30 A.M., the first Allied troops and tanks were landed. Some got no farther than the beach. Some were drowned leaving the landing crafts. But still others got through. All day long they kept coming and dying, fighting their way grimly through the mines and barbed wire and the machine gun fire that raked the beach. But they held on and established a beachhead. Hitler's Europe had been invaded.

Some soldiers made it only as far as the beach. They paved the way for those who came after. This picture was captioned with a soldier's remembrance of the day: "Whenever anyone mentions Omaha Beach, I always think of running by that dead GI and wondering if I was going to get it."

THE BATTLE FOR FRANCE

The next step for the Allies was to extend their beachhead and break through the German fortifications. The port city of Cherbourg was wrested from the Germans on June 26. Although the Germans destroyed most of it, it was in working order again by the beginning of August. This gave the Allies a port through which to pour more troops and supplies into France.

Normandy, the part of France where the invasion forces had landed, had terrain that slowed troop movements. Ridges of very dense hedges crisscrossed Normandy, so thick that even tanks had difficulty breaking through them. One Allied soldier found a way to adapt his tank to the difficult conditions. He attached a metal piece from the German landing obstacles to the front of his tank. When the tank struck the hedges, the metal tore a hole in the hedge. The adaptation was ordered for all the tanks, and the Allies swept onward.

The Allied advance divided into two thrusts. One under British General Montgomery engaged the main body of German troops around Caen on July 20. In the west, the second thrust, using primarily American troops, was to break out of Normandy to the south and then circle east moving toward the Seine River. This second thrust broke out on July 28 and reached the coastal town of St. Nazaire. Commanded by General George Patton, the Americans now swung east, encircling and capturing 100,000 German defenders. The larger body of German troops fled eastward across the Seine, pursued by Patton's forces.

Fighting in northern France had resulted in almost half a million German casualties. Allied losses were about half that. The supply situation was now crucial. The Germans held desperately onto their other port cities so that the Allies would have trouble supporting all the troops they had landed in France. Some of the advancing armies slowed their drives eastward.

On August 5, Allied troops based in Italy made a second landing in the south of France. With the Germans pinned down in the north, the second group of invaders made rapid progress. By September 11, they linked up with Patton's army moving eastward.

Eisenhower's plan in France was to weaken the German armies as much as possible. He decided to cut into the German armies in the countryside. Free French units under General Jacques Leclerc and resistance fighters attacked the Germans holding Paris. The capital of France was back in French hands on August 25, 1944. By mid-September most of France was in Allied hands.

Above: in the French city of Luxeuil, liberated by the invasion force coming from the south, an American GI accepts a present from a grateful resident. Below: this woman was accused of collaborating with the Germans during the occupation of France. When the Germans left, such people were rounded up and had their heads shaved as a mark of disgrace.

Arnhem

Eisenhower desperately needed more supplies before he could begin another offensive. He decided to allow Montgomery to try a daring attack northward to clear the Belgian port of Antwerp. Antwerp had been captured by the British in the middle of September. But the area around it in Belgium and northern Holland was still held by the Germans, making the port unusable. The available supplies were sent to Montgomery in preparation for the drive north.

On September 17, British and Polish troops parachuted into Arnhem, Holland, six miles (9.5 km.) west of the city. They were surprised by a larger force of Germans than they had expected. In addition, bad weather kept Montgomery from breaking through to Arnhem from the south. After desperate fighting, the Germans overran the Allied paratroopers and regained control of Arnhem.

In November and early December, Montgomery's troops in heavy fighting broke through the Scheldt River area around Antwerp and cleared it of German troops. It was November 28 before the Allies could begin using the port.

THE RUSSIAN OFFENSIVES

Hitler was now fighting what the Germans had always dreaded—a two-front war. In Russia, on the Eastern Front, Hitler's generals wanted to pull back and build stronger defensive positions. Once more, Hitler refused to allow any retreat. He threw precious reserve troops into the front lines, sacrificing them before the relentless Russian advance.

Hitler moved the reserves into southern Poland, expecting the next Russian attack to come there. Instead, the Russian strike in June 1944, was in the north of Poland. With a massive attack, the Russians blasted a hole 250 miles (400 km.) wide and 250 miles (400 km.) deep in the German lines. A new German commander, General Walther Model, managed to regroup what was left of the German armies. They made another stand just east of the Polish capital of Warsaw.

As the Russians engaged the Germans near Warsaw in early August, the Polish citizens of the city rose in rebellion against the Nazis. They had secretly organized and collected weapons. With the help of the Russians, they hoped to drive out the Germans.

But the Russians held back. Stalin knew of the uprising, but he knew that the Polish underground was loyal to the non-Communist Polish government that had escaped to England. Stalin wanted a Communist government to take over Poland, and he let the Germans crush the rebellion and exterminate the non-Communist opposition. The Russians finally took Warsaw in January of 1945.

In the heart of Germany, Hitler had survived an assassination attempt by some of his generals in July 1944. A bomb was planted in his headquarters, and only luck saved Hitler from destruction. The German officers who planned a takeover of the government were tortured and executed.

Now the Russians swept south into the Balkans, taking most of Rumania and Bulgaria in August and September 1944. In the north, they launched another attack on Finland, forcing the Finns to sign a surrender in September. At the end of October they entered East Prussia. Here they were brought to a halt by fanatical German defenders.

Below: the V-1 was a large bomb propelled by a jet engine. The terrible screeching noise the weapons made gave only a few seconds warning. Soon after the Allies reached Normandy, they captured the coastal launching sites of the V-1 rockets. Left: in September 1944, Hitler unveiled the V-2. A true rocket, which flew above the atmosphere so that it made no sound, the V-2 had a greater range than the V-1. The V-2s rained silent death down on England and Antwerp.

THE GERMAN COUNTEROFFENSIVE

Hitler now unveiled the secret weapons he had promised the German people. They were rocket bombs: the V-1, which began falling on Britain in June 1944; and the V-2, which was used on England and the Allied port of Antwerp. More than two-thirds of Antwerp was destroyed in the bombings, but the V-weapons failed to turn the tide.

Hitler now decided to rally his forces for a counterattack on the Allies. The plan looked good, on paper. It was basically the same plan that had defeated France in 1940. The Germans would strike through the Ardennes, cut the Allies in two, and fight their way to Antwerp and the sea. The *Panzer* divisions would lead the Germans once again in a massive *Blitzkrieg*.

But in 1940 France was weak and Hitler's forces were stronger, fresh, and well-supplied. The German *Luftwaffe* had been unchallenged in the air and able to provide massive air support. Now, the Allies had the superior forces. Germany had lost control of the skies. Hitler's troops had been decimated by fighting on all fronts.

Nevertheless, when the German counterattack began in the middle of December 1944, it did tear a hole in the Allied lines. The best units of Hitler's army led the way. Bad weather kept the Allied air support from aiding the defenders. German soldiers in American uniforms were dropped behind the lines to spread confusion among the Allies. By December 21, the Germans had advanced almost 60 miles (96 km.). The American forces kept the Germans pressed in on a narrow front, and the advance showed on the map as a bulge westward. The offensive became known as the "Battle of the Bulge."

An American soldier holds his rifle on two German prisoners taken during the Battle of the Bulge.

An American tank burns as this Nazi soldier looks bleakly at his chances for survival. Hitler had said earlier, "We may be destroyed, but if we are, we shall drag a world with us—a world in flames."

In the middle of the bulge was the city of Bastogne, still held by surrounded American troops. The Germans called for the Americans to surrender. The American commanding general sent back the message, "Nuts."

When the weather cleared, Allied air support helped to halt the German advance. Tank divisions led by American General Patton rescued Bastogne. The Germans, short of supplies, fuel, and fresh reserves, were slowly driven back. Hitler had sacrificed 200,000 of his best troops—and failed. There were no replacements left.

THE RACE TO THE RHINE

In the fall of 1944, the Allies had made some advances into Germany itself. On October 21, Aachen fell; November 2, Metz; Strasbourg, November 26.

In February 1945, Eisenhower directed a massive advance against the German fortifications known as the Siegfried Line. He wanted to take advantage of the German weaknesses caused by the Battle of the Bulge. Beyond the Siegfried Line lay the Rhine River, a great natural barrier guarding the interior of Germany. In four weeks of fighting the Allies broke the Siegfried Line and advanced to the Rhine.

A Russian slave worker transported to Germany and liberated by advancing American troops. He is pointing out one of the Nazi guards who brutally beat the prisoners.

Below: the bridge at Remagen, whose capture intact saved the Allies many
decisive days in their drive on Berlin. Above: a Russian soldier in East Prussia.
German resistance stiffened as Russian troops advanced into Germany.

Hitler had given orders that all bridges over the Rhine were to be destroyed. But General Omar Bradley's forces moved quickly, and the bridge at Remagen was captured intact on March 7. Hitler ordered the commanders responsible hanged, but the Allies swept across the bridge and established a defensive position on the other side.

Some American and British commanders now argued for a deep, narrow thrust into Germany, aiming at Berlin. But such a strategy would have risked encirclement by Germans breaking through the line. Eisenhower ordered a broad front across Germany. He was concerned with destroying the troops and industrial capacity of Germany. By April, the Ruhr Valley, the heart of Germany's industrial might, was in Allied hands.

Some of Eisenhower's commanders wished to drive on Berlin because it was the capital. But Eisenhower knew that the Big Three had already established zones of control in Germany for after the war. He was content to allow the Russians to take on the bloody task of capturing Berlin.

The Russians moved through Poland to the Oder River, 30 miles (48 km.) from Berlin. The Germans defended this line so fiercely that the Russians were thrown back. In February 1945, the Russians took Budapest, Hungary after a long siege. In the south, the Russians captured Vienna, the capital of Austria, on April 13. But in mid-April, the Oder River line still held.

THE YALTA CONFERENCE

Roosevelt, Churchill, and Stalin met at the Russian city of Yalta in February 1945. It was clear by that time that Germany would be defeated soon. Stalin was determined that Eastern Europe would fall under Russian influence and that the German nation would be divided. Roosevelt was concerned with the war in Asia. It had been estimated that an attack on the islands of Japan would cost over a million casualties. Roosevelt wanted Stalin to enter the war against Japan. In return, he was willing to make concessions. The agreements at Yalta allowed the Russians to have their influence in Eastern Europe. In the Far East, the Russians were given concessions in Manchuria, at the expense of China.

German soldiers at the end of the war using horse-drawn carts to flee the oncoming Soviet troops. All the fuel supplies to operate tanks and trucks had been depleted.

THE FALL OF BERLIN

Hitler ordered the Germans to fight to the last man. The Russians assembled a massive force to break the Oder River line. In six days, they had crushed the resisting Germans and advanced to Berlin. The last desperate Germans, civilians and twelve-year-old "soldiers" included, made the Russians pay for every city block. In return, the Russians took terrible vengeance on the populace. Hitler directed the German forces from his bomb shelter within the city.

To the south, American troops linked up with the advancing Russians on the Elbe River on April 18. While the fighting was going on, Roosevelt died on April 12. His name appeared in the casualty lists along with the others who had died that day: "Roosevelt, Franklin D., commander in chief."

On April 30, with the Russians only blocks away, Hitler committed suicide. On May 7, General Alfred Jodl signed the unconditional surrender of the German army. Eisenhower sent a telegram to headquarters: "The mission of this Allied Force was fulfilled at 3:00 A.M., local time, 7 May 1945. Eisenhower."

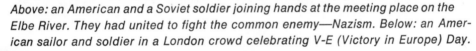

Above: an American and a Soviet soldier joining hands at the meeting place on the Elbe River. They had united to fight the common enemy—Nazism. Below: an American sailor and soldier in a London crowd celebrating V-E (Victory in Europe) Day.

Left: Jews, like this old woman, were required to wear the Star of David as a badge of identification in Hitler's Reich. When this regulation was enforced in occupied Denmark, the king appeared wearing a Star, and his subjects got the message—from then on, everyone wore them. Above: American troops at some camps went to the nearest German village and made the townspeople walk through to see the crime of the German nation.

Right: starved prisoners, nearly dead from hunger, at one of the largest Nazi concentration camps located in Evensee, Austria. Inmates were dying at the rate of two thousand a week just from starvation.

THE FINAL SOLUTION

As the victorious Allies made their way across Europe, they discovered the most horrifying deed of Hitler's Third Reich. In small towns whose names were soon to haunt the world—Auschwitz, Belsen, Maidanek, Buchenwald, Dachau—they found concentration camps whose inmates had been sent from all over Europe to become slaves, to be tortured, and to be put to death. The starved, ghastly mistreated victims who were still alive shocked the liberating armies. But the piles of corpses the Nazis had not managed to dispose of horrified the world. As the tales of mass exterminations became known, the Allies' feelings turned to revulsion for the German people who had allowed such crimes to happen.

Yet Hitler had made known all along his intentions for the Jews, Gypsies, Slavs, and other so-called "inferior" peoples. From the beginning, he had made the Jews scapegoats for all of Germany's ills. In 1939, he told the German Reichstag of his plans for "the obliteration of the Jewish race." As the Nazis captured Poland, with its 3 million Jews, and parts of Russia, with another 3 million, and western Europe with half a million more, his plans did not change.

The tragedy was that in Germany in particular Jews had played an important role in society. Many Jews were doctors, scientists, lawyers, and teachers. Early in Hitler's regime, they were separated from their positions in society. Those who could, escaped to England, the United States, and other free countries. When the war broke out, Hitler rounded up and imprisoned all who could not escape.

In 1942, a Nazi directive called for the complete elimination of the Jewish people. They were then sent to the death camps where whole sections of Hitler's Nazi SS were devoted to the logistical problems of killing and disposing of millions of human beings.

In some regions of Eastern Europe the Jewish populations resisted. In Warsaw, the Jewish ghetto—the section of the city where Jews were required to live—rose in open revolt in April 1943. The Jews put up a heroic resistance using hand grenades and homemade weapons against tanks and artillery. Hitler's storm troopers brutally crushed the revolt and virtually annihilated the population.

In the west of Europe, non-Jewish citizens, particularly in Denmark and Holland, tried to protect the Jews. People lent their houses as hiding places, and helped Jews escape to neutral countries.

But more than 6 million Jews were killed by Hitler during the war. It was a crime that was to haunt the civilized world, and shake people's faith in humanity itself.

THE ASIAN WAR 1942–1945

ISLAND HOPPING

After the defeat of the Japanese at Midway, the Allies had to plan their counterattack. The Japanese had fortified such key islands as Rabaul near New Guinea and Truk in the Carolines. The Allied strategy was to avoid the most strongly defended islands, "hopping" the places where Japanese strength was greatest. By attacking weaker islands behind the strong points, the Japanese supply lines could be cut off.

The Allies made two major thrusts toward Japan. One went east from New Guinea to the Philippines, and from there north to Japan. The other, much longer line ran all the way across tiny Pacific islands whose names were known only to geographers before they became major battle sites.

Guadalcanal

When the Japanese planned to build up the island of Guadalcanal in the Solomon chain east of New Guinea as a strong defensive point, the Americans decided to stop them. American landings were made on Guadalcanal on August 7, 1942. American marines seized a partially completed Japanese airfield, which they renamed Henderson Field. This spot was the crux of six months of bitter fighting. Both sides tested the other's strength and will to fight at Guadalcanal.

Night after night, Japanese ships came down the slot between the Solomon Islands to bombard the marines at Henderson Field. Numerous fanatical Japanese troops tried to break the marines' hold on the now-precious airstrip. Six times, American naval forces went up the slot to knock out the Japanese naval bases. Finally, after six months of bitter and bloody fighting, the marines controlled the island. Japanese ships evacuated what remained of their ground troops, and retreated up the slot for the last time.

Above: amphibious vehicles called "Ducks" loaded with ammunition hit the water off Guadalcanal on their way to a ship anchored offshore. Below: repairs being made on the artificial runway at Henderson Field after a Japanese bombing raid. Seabees (for Construction Battalions—CBs) were responsible for this type of construction and repair in combat zones, and their work included some of the most difficult and hazardous tasks of the war.

Japanese defenders at Buna who followed the code of dying rather than surrender.

In all the island hopping, beginning with Guadalcanal, one of the toughest jobs of the American troops was to clean the jungle islands of defending Japanese troops. The Japanese regarded it as dishonorable to surrender, and the fighting in each island was prolonged and costly in terms of lives.

New Guinea

New Guinea is a large island north of Australia. If it fell to the Japanese, they would have a base from which to mount an invasion of Australia itself. The earlier attempt of the Japanese to take the strategic town of Port Moresby in eastern New Guinea had failed. The task of defending New Guinea was assigned to General Douglas MacArthur. Many of his troops were hard-fighting Australians who had returned from the desert fighting against Rommel.

Japanese positions on the northern coast of New Guinea were MacArthur's target. After routing the Japanese from the eastern peninsula area of Papua in January 1943, MacArthur drove westward across the island. With invaluable help from Admiral William Halsey's aircraft carriers and planes, MacArthur had secured the island by the summer of 1944. Throughout the New Guinea campaign, Allied victories had depended on the coordination of land, sea, and air forces. Both MacArthur and Halsey were skilled at such coordination. The only comparable Japanese officer was Admiral Yamamoto, and he had been killed in 1943 when his plane was shot down by American fighter aircraft from Henderson Field.

[84]

Leapfrogging the Pacific

The island hopping now started in earnest, with intense fighting over each tiny rock. In November 1943, Americans attacked Makin and Tarawa islands in the Gilbert chain. Almost 1,000 Americans were killed in the bloody fighting. Using air support based on Tarawa, the Americans took Kwajalein in the Marshalls in February 1944.

With the additional air bases, the Americans began concentrated bombing attacks on the two strong Japanese bases of Truk and Rabaul. In two days, American planes dropped thirty times as much explosives on Truk as the Japanese had dropped on Pearl Harbor. Both bases were knocked out of the war.

On the fifteenth of June, 1943, American marines began their attack on Saipan in the southern Marianas. When a Japanese fleet came to the rescue, combined American air, surface, and undersea forces sank three carriers and shot down 300 Japanese planes. American pilots called this the "Great Marianas Turkey Shoot." The Japanese ashore still resisted fiercely. They lost almost 24,000 men defending Saipan. But by August Saipan and two other islands in the Marianas, Guam and Tinian, were controlled by the Americans.

Many of the Pacific islands were mountainous. Japanese troops, such as the artillery squads shown at left, used the terrain well for a long, drawn-out resistance. Right: "mopping-up" operations. These two marines have just tossed a charge of high explosives into a Japanese dugout to make sure it was cleared of defenders.

Left: a kamikaze attack on the American ship St. Lo during the Battle of Leyte Gulf. The pilot scored a direct hit. The role of the kamikaze, or "divine wind," was regarded as one of the highest nobility by the Japanese. In ceremonies before their missions, kamikaze pilots sometimes cut off a finger to be sent home to their families as a remembrance. Right: the fighting on Corregidor was exceptionally bloody. Americans re-taking the island remembered the Bataan Death March that the Japanese had sent American prisoners on when the island had fallen to the Japanese at the beginning of the war. Below: civilians caught in the fighting between Americans and Japanese in Manila are led out of a building that had been damaged by shelling. Extensive firing in Manila killed or injured many civilians.

The Battle of Leyte Gulf

The Americans now prepared for a return to the Philippines. For six weeks, American ships and planes bombarded Japanese bases that could support Japanese defenders in the Philippine Islands. More than 2,000 Japanese planes were destroyed, 450 ships damaged, and many more supply depots, airfields, and naval installations smashed.

On October 20 began the greatest naval battle in history. The invasion forces were carried and protected by 700 American ships. The Japanese troops ashore were ordered to resist the invasion at all costs. The Japanese navy, short of planes by now, divided into three segments. A northern force was to be used as a decoy. The central force would bear the brunt of the initial attack, and a southern force would stand by to reinforce areas that required assistance.

On October 23, Halsey's Third Fleet attacked the central force and sank two ships. The next day, more central force ships suffered damage, and the southern force was almost annihilated. But then Halsey was distracted by the dummy northern force. He set off in pursuit. On October 25, the central force, which had been damaged but not destroyed, as Halsey had thought, came steaming toward the American beachhead where MacArthur and 100,000 troops were without naval or air support—completely at the mercy of the Japanese fleet.

A makeshift force of small escort carriers under Admiral Clifton Sprague moved in between the Japanese and the beaches. Using delaying tactics, smoke screens, and what little firepower he could muster, Admiral Sprague held off the Japanese for a crucial three hours. In desperation, the Japanese turned to *kamikaze* attacks. In these, a Japanese pilot used his plane to crash directly into the deck of an American ship. Such suicide attacks had their counterpart on land with the *banzai* attacks of Japanese troops who ran head on into American machine guns and artillery, hoping to overrun the position by sheer determination.

Five of Admiral Sprague's ships were sunk, and there was little chance he could have held off the stronger Japanese much longer. But suddenly the Japanese turned and fled, apparently fearing that reinforcements were on the way.

Unknown to the Americans at the time, the Japanese had no reserve naval forces left. It would have been relatively easy to commence the invasion of Japan itself. But the fighting went on grimly in the Philippines, with the main island, Luzon, falling in early 1945.

A Chinese bazooka assault team are properly camouflaged for their task.

THE WAR IN MAINLAND ASIA

On the Allied side, the war in mainland Asia was complicated by the confusion of command. The burden of the Pacific war fell almost entirely on the Americans, with some Australian support. Britain, however, had interests in the Far East that required British troop support.

The main concern of the Allies was to keep the Burma Road open from China to India. If the Chinese forces could be kept supplied through the Burma Road lifeline, precious Japanese troop strength would be spent fighting the Chinese.

Though the Japanese were skilled jungle fighters, they never had sufficient strength to control the vast population of China and the other countries of mainland Asia. American General "Vinegar Joe" Stilwell led American-trained Chinese divisions in the northeast of Burma. To the west, British Lord Mountbatten, who feared not only the loss of Burma but a potential Japanese advance into India, commanded the combined Allied forces. Colorful generals such as British General Orde Wingate, with his "Chindits," and American General Frank Merrill, with his "Merrill's Marauders," led specially trained units that harassed the Japanese in guerrilla-war fashion. The Allies also trained groups in guerrilla tactics to help them raid the Japanese invaders.

[88]

The air war chiefly involved the bombing of Japanese bases. The Allies' difficulty here was in establishing their own bases close enough to be effective. Propeller-driven aircraft, even the "long-range" bombers, couldn't cover the vast distances necessary. The same problem applied to supplies that had to be parachuted to troops far inland. The shortest route to China from India was over the Himalayas, the world's highest mountains. The pilots who flew this route, including General Claire Chennault's Flying Tigers, called it "the Hump."

Surmounting all these problems of support and the terrible conditions of jungle fighting, the Allies nonetheless had retaken Burma by 1944. A supply line for the Chinese was maintained throughout the war. The Japanese hold on Manchuria and China was not broken until the very end, however. On the day before the war ended, Russia finally declared war on Japan, and Russian troops occupied Manchuria.

A Chinese tank moves down the Burma road throught a battered Burmese village. The war raging around them never stopped for the civilian population. It destroyed their homes, farms, shops, and temples. Millions fled, but there was no place to go where the war might not come next.

THE DEFEAT OF JAPAN

The Air War

Lack of bases close enough to support bombers kept the Americans from hitting the home islands of Japan. But with the Allied victories in the Pacific of 1943 and 1944, they seized air fields from which long-range bombers could operate against Tokyo.

As the war continued, the Japanese air force became less and less effective. Pilots and planes lost in the great battles of 1943 and 1944 were not easily replaced. The industrial might of the United States continued to pour supplies and equipment into the Pacific war. Eventually, American planes could fly over Japan virtually unchallenged. They began to carry greater amounts of bombs, and the destruction was devastating. Tokyo, Osaka, and most other cities suffered great damage, as did the industrial sites within Japan.

The Last Islands

The island of Iwo Jima was one of the last defensive points of Japan. Radar and fighter planes based here offered little resistance to the American Superfortress bombers. Yet after seven months of heavy bombing against the tiny island, Iwo Jima still operated effectively. The Americans decided that Iwo must be taken. On February 19, 1945, American troops landed on the island.

In one of the most famous photographs of the war, U.S. Marines raise the flag on the summit of Mount Suribachi on Iwo Jima. Marine General "Howlin' Mad" Smith said that the fighting on Iwo was the toughest any Marine had ever faced in the history of the Corps.

Marines passing the body of a dead Japanese soldier on Okinawa. Suicide missions and decoys were common here, and combat veterans looked twice to make sure an enemy was dead.

Awaiting them were 23,000 crack Japanese troops and heavy concrete fortifications. Overlooking the eight-square-mile (20-sq.-km.) island was the volcanic mountain of Suribachi. Fighting there was heaviest as the Americans inched their way to the summit. Japanese artillery and machine guns raked the attacking Americans in a savage defensive action. Finally, on February 23, the Americans took the summit. On March 16, the island was in American hands, though scattered defenders continued to operate for months.

The island of Okinawa in the Ryukyu chain was close to Japan itself. It would provide a springboard for the final invasion of Japan, if the Allies could subdue its defenders. On the morning of April 1, 1945, supported by more than 1,450 ships and 1,500 carrier-based planes, American troops came ashore at Okinawa. The desperate Japanese defense of the island made the greatest use so far of the *kamikaze,* or suicide missions. Planes and boats alike were sent hurtling against American support ships and landing craft. Ashore, the Americans ran into heavy artillery fire and tropical rains which bogged the island in mud. In three months of fighting on Okinawa, the Japanese suffered more than 100,000 men killed. Americans lost 7,613 dead in the fighting. On June 21, organized Japanese resistance collapsed with the suicide of the Japanese commander. As at Iwo Jima, Japanese stragglers continued harassment of the Americans till the end of the war.

The Atomic Bomb

The next step in the Pacific was to be the invasion of Japan itself. The bloody fighting and the refusal of most Japanese soldiers to surrender had convinced the Americans that the invasion of Japan would be costly. Estimates of casualties ranged above a million men.

The new American president, Harry Truman, had been told of secret United States efforts to build a superweapon. At the beginning of the war, a refugee German Jewish scientist had written President Roosevelt a letter. The scientist, Albert Einstein, described the possibility of a bomb of terrific power. This was the atomic bomb. In secret discussions among American scientists, the possibility was raised that Germany might already be working on such a bomb. Einstein and other refugee scientists knew that the Axis powers had the technology to build such a bomb.

On Roosevelt's directive, the Manhattan Project was set up to develop the superbomb. Throughout the war, the scientists working on the bomb saw themselves racing against the Germans' efforts. In fact, Hitler had taken little interest in such a project and had not devoted the vast resources necessary to develop the bomb. During the war, the United States spent more than $2,000,000,000 on the Manhattan Project.

The bomb was ready at last. In great secrecy, it was tested in the desert area of New Mexico on July 16, 1945. The devastation it caused was almost beyond belief. But by then Germany had been defeated by conventional means. The scientists who had worked on the bomb had done so to fight the evil that Hitler represented. They were hesitant about using it against the Japanese. Some of them advised Truman to keep the bomb a secret, in reserve. But Truman knew the great losses that a conventional invasion of Japan would bring. He issued an ultimatum to the Japanese government: surrender or face destruction. They did not respond to Truman's demand.

At the direction of Truman and Prime Minister Churchill, on August 6, 1945, the American bomber *Enola Gay* dropped an atomic bomb on the Japanese city of Hiroshima. Three days later a second bomb was dropped on the city of Nagasaki. Both cities were utterly destroyed. Many of the Japanese who were not killed outright died later, sometimes years later, from burns and the harmful radioactive effects of the bomb.

On August 15, the emperor of Japan told his people that the war was over.

Left: a nuclear weapon of the type dropped over Hiroshima. The 9,000-pound (over 4,000 kg.) atomic bomb measured 28 inches (72 cm.) in diameter and 120 inches (305 cm.) in length. Below: Nagasaki after the blast. The wooden shacks were rebuilt after the bomb. More than 39,000 people were killed and 25,000 severely wounded in the first seconds of the explosion. Above: when the Emperor of Japan spoke on the radio to announce that the war was over, his subjects knelt before his voice, which most of them had never heard. The people gathered here are weeping at the message.

INDEX